MADEIRA

COMPREHENSIVE GUIDE TRAVEL 2024 AND BEYOND

The Definitive Handbook to Madeira's Timeless Charms, Unveiling Unmissable Experiences, Expert Insights, and Future Treasures – Packed with Detailed Maps, Travel Planner and 2024 Imagery Calendar

BY

TARA WARREN

Copyright © 2024 TARA D. WARREN. This extensive travel guide titled **"MADEIRA COMPREHENSIVE TRAVEL GUIDE 2024 AND BEYOND"** is safeguarded by global copyright regulations. All rights are reserved, encompassing reproduction, distribution, or transmission of any part of this guide in any form without explicit written consent from the author. Unauthorized utilization or replication of this travel guide is explicitly forbidden and may lead to legal consequences. Your consideration for the author's creative endeavour is sincerely valued.

Table of Contents

Copyright... 1
My Experience in Madeira...5
Madeira FAQs?...7
Why Visit Madeira?.. 10
What to Expect from this Guide......................................13

CHAPTER 1. INTRODUCTION TO MADEIRA.................... 16
1.1 History and Heritage.. 16
1.2 Geography and Climate... 19
1.3 Local Customs and Traditions....................................21
1.4 Madeira in the Present...23
1.5 Getting to Know the Locals.......................................26

CHAPTER 2. ACCOMMODATION OPTIONS........................ 29
2.1 Hotels and Resorts..29
2.2 Guesthouses and Bed & Breakfasts......................... 32
2.3 Vacation Rentals..34
2.4 Camping Sites..36
2.5 Unique Stays and Boutique Hotels...........................38

CHAPTER 3. TRANSPORTATION IN MADEIRA................. 41
3.1 Getting to Madeira.. 41
3.2 Public Transportation...43
3.3 Car Rentals and Driving Tips.................................... 45
3.4 Taxis and Ride-Sharing... 48
3.5 Navigating Madeira's Roads......................................50

CHAPTER 4. TOP ATTRACTIONS..53
4.1 Must-Visit Landmarks.. 53
4.2 Natural Wonders...55

4.3 Museums and Galleries...58

4.4 Hidden Gems.. 59

4.5 Local Festivals and Events...61

CHAPTER 5. PRACTICAL INFORMATION AND TRAVEL RESOURCES.. 65

5.1 Maps and Navigation..65

5.2 Essential Packing List.. 67

5.3 Safety Tips and Emergency Contacts..................................... 70

5.4 Currency, Banking, Budgeting and Money Matters............... 72

5.5 Language, Communication and Useful Phrases....................74

5.6 Useful Websites, Mobile Apps and Online Resources...........77

5.7 Visitor Centers and Tourist Assistance...................................79

CHAPTER 6. CULINARY DELIGHTS.. 82

6.1 Traditional Madeiran Cuisine...82

6.2 Popular Dishes and Snacks...85

6.3 Dining Etiquette... 87

6.4 Recommended Restaurants..90

6.5 Food Festivals and Markets.. 92

CHAPTER 7. CULTURE AND HERITAGE.. 95

7.1 Arts and Crafts...95

7.2 Historical Sites... 98

7.3 Local Art Scene..101

7.4 Traditional Music and Dance... 103

7.5 Celebrating Madeiran Culture..106

CHAPTER 8. OUTDOOR ACTIVITIES AND ADVENTURES...................109

8.1 Hiking and Trekking Trails..109

8.2 Water Sports.. 112

8.3 Bird Watching.. 115

8.4 Golf Courses..117

8.5 Exploring Madeira's Natural Beauty...119

8.6 Family and Kids Friendly Activities.. 122

8.7 Activities for Solo Travelers... 125

CHAPTER 9. SHOPPING IN MADEIRA................................... 128

9.1 Souvenirs and Local Crafts... 128

9.2 Markets and Shopping Districts... 131

9.3 Specialty Stores... 133

9.4 Fashion and Design... 136

9.5 Tips for Bargain Hunting... 138

CHAPTER 10. DAY TRIPS AND EXCURSIONS............................ 142

10.1 Nearby Islands..142

10.2 Scenic Drives.. 145

10.3 Historical Day Trips... 147

10.4 Adventure Day Excursions... 150

10.5 Relaxing Getaways.. 152

CHAPTER 11. ENTERTAINMENT AND NIGHTLIFE........................156

11.1 Bars and Pubs..156

11.2 Nightclubs... 159

11.3 Live Music Venues.. 161

11.4 Cultural Performances.. 164

11.5 Festivals and Celebrations... 166

CONCLUSION AND INSIDER TIPS FOR VISITORS......................... 170

MADEIRA TRAVEL PLANNER AND 2024 CALENDAR........................ 173

MY EXPERIENCE IN MADEIRA

Embarking on my journey to Madeira was not merely a destination on my travel itinerary; it unfolded as an odyssey, a profound exploration that etched memories on the canvas of my soul. As a seasoned traveler and author, I have always believed in the power of first-hand experiences, in allowing the heart to guide the pen, and in crafting narratives that extend beyond the confines of book pages. Madeira, with its unparalleled beauty and cultural richness, welcomed me with an embrace that transcended the ordinary. From the very moment I set foot on this verdant oasis in the Atlantic, I sensed an otherworldly charm that set it apart from any other destination I had encountered.

The journey began in Funchal, the capital city, where cobbled streets echoed the footsteps of generations past. As a traveler with a penchant for history, these streets became my time machine, guiding me through a tapestry of Portuguese and Moorish influences. The São Tiago Fortress, standing stoically, narrated tales of maritime exploits and the island's resilient spirit.

Venturing into the heart of Madeira's natural wonders became an adventure that unfolded with every step. Hiking trails led me to breathtaking viewpoints, unveiling panoramas of rugged terrain, serene forests, and cascading waterfalls. The Laurissilva Forest, a testament to time's passage, enveloped me in its ancient embrace, while Levada walks offered a tranquil journey through the island's irrigation channels, exposing landscapes of untouched beauty.

Culinary exploration emerged as a central theme of my Madeiran sojourn. The island's cuisine, a delightful fusion of flavors, tantalized my taste buds with local delicacies like espetada and the exotic sweetness of passion fruit.

Each meal was not just sustenance; it was a passage into the heart of Madeiran culture, often shared in family-owned restaurants that exuded warmth and authenticity.

Connecting with the island's locals elevated my experience to a level beyond mere tourism. Conversations in cafes, encounters in small villages, and shared laughter revealed a community proud of their island and eager to share its wonders. The personal interactions transformed my journey from a sightseeing expedition into a genuine cultural exchange.

Navigating Madeira's coastal beauty became an ethereal experience, especially during the mesmerizing sunsets. Sailing along the cliffs, witnessing the sky ablaze with hues of pink and gold, left an indelible mark on my memory. It was a moment of serenity that transcended the everyday, inviting contemplation and connection with nature.

Madeira's festivals and traditions, a vibrant tapestry woven through time, beckoned me to participate in its celebrations. From the spirited Carnival to the timeless Festa da Flor, the island revealed itself as a living canvas of music, dance, and cultural expressions. In those moments, I became not just an observer but a participant in the heartbeat of Madeira.

Modeira is an invitation to fellow wanderers to go beyond the guidebooks, to explore the hidden corners, and to embrace the warmth of Madeira's people. The island, with its enchanting allure, promises an adventure that resonates in the heart long after the journey concludes. As a traveler and storyteller, I extend the invitation: let Madeira capture your imagination, let its landscapes etch themselves into your soul, and let the echoes of its culture resonate in your heart.

MADEIRA FAQS?

1. What is the best time to visit Madeira?
Madeira boasts a mild climate year-round, but the best time to visit is during the spring (April to June) or fall (September to November) when temperatures are pleasant, and the island is less crowded.

2. How do I get to Madeira?
Madeira is accessible by air. The Cristiano Ronaldo International Airport in Funchal welcomes flights from major European cities. Direct flights and connections are available.

3. What are the accommodation options in Madeira?
Accommodation choices vary, ranging from luxury hotels and resorts in Funchal to charming guest houses in rural areas. Vacation rentals and boutique hotels offer diverse options for every traveler.

4. Do I need a rental car in Madeira?
While public transportation is available, renting a car provides flexibility to explore the island's remote corners. The roads are well-maintained, and the scenic drives are worth experiencing.

5. What are the must-visit attractions in Madeira?
Key attractions include the Laurissilva Forest, Pico do Arieiro, and the historic town of Funchal. Nature reserves, botanical gardens, and traditional villages are also worth exploring.

6. Are there hiking opportunities in Madeira?

Absolutely. Madeira is a hiker's paradise, with a network of trails offering diverse landscapes. From challenging hikes to leisurely strolls along levadas, there's something for every skill level.

7. What is the local cuisine like?

Madeiran cuisine is a delightful blend of Portuguese and island flavors. Try local dishes like Espetada, Black Scabbardfish, and indulge in the famous Madeira wine.

8. Is English widely spoken in Madeira?

Yes, English is widely spoken, especially in tourist areas. However, learning a few Portuguese phrases can enhance the overall experience and interactions with locals.

9. Are there any cultural events in Madeira?

Madeira hosts various cultural events throughout the year, including the Carnival, Flower Festival, and Wine Festival. Check the calendar to align your visit with these vibrant celebrations.

10. How safe is Madeira for tourists?

Madeira is considered safe for tourists. The crime rate is low, and locals are welcoming. Exercise standard safety precautions and be mindful of natural elements during outdoor activities.

11. Are credit cards widely accepted?

Credit cards are generally accepted in hotels, restaurants, and larger establishments. However, it's advisable to carry some cash, especially in more remote areas.

12. What outdoor activities are popular in Madeira?

Madeira offers a plethora of outdoor activities, including hiking, canyoning, whale watching, and water sports like snorkeling and diving.

13. How is the public transportation system?

Madeira has a reliable public transportation system, including buses and taxis. However, renting a car is recommended for more extensive exploration.

14. Can I take day trips to nearby islands?

Yes, day trips to nearby Porto Santo or Desertas Islands are popular. Ferry services and guided tours are available for those seeking island-hopping adventures.

15. What souvenirs can I buy in Madeira?

Traditional Madeiran crafts, embroidery, Madeira wine, and local delicacies make for excellent souvenirs. Explore markets and specialty stores for unique finds.

WHY VISIT MADEIRA?

As a seasoned traveler and devoted author, my wanderlust has taken me to diverse corners of the globe. However, there are certain places that etch themselves into the fabric of your being, creating an indelible connection. Madeira, the pearl of the Atlantic, is one such destination that beckons with a unique allure, inviting travelers to embark on a journey of unparalleled beauty, rich culture, and unforgettable experiences.

A Symphony of Nature's Beauty

Madeira's landscapes unfold like a masterpiece, each stroke painted with the vibrant hues of nature. The island is a haven of biodiversity, boasting lush forests, dramatic cliffs, and cascading waterfalls. As a traveler who cherishes the embrace of nature, Madeira offers a symphony of experiences – from traversing the ancient Laurissilva Forest, a UNESCO World Heritage site, to meandering along the iconic levadas that crisscross the island. The panoramic vistas, with the Atlantic as a backdrop, evoke a sense of awe and wonder.

Unveiling Hidden Gems and Charming Villages

Beyond the postcard-perfect scenes lies a tapestry of hidden gems and charming villages, each with its own story to tell. Exploring the cobbled streets of Funchal, the capital city, is like stepping into a living history book, where centuries-old architecture stands as a testament to the island's storied past. Venturing into the smaller villages reveals the heart of Madeira – where locals welcome visitors with open arms, sharing tales of tradition, and inviting them to partake in the island's timeless culture.

Culinary Delights and the Art of Slow Living

Madeira's culinary scene is a celebration of flavors that transcend the ordinary. From succulent espetada skewers to the unique Black Scabbardfish, each dish is a journey into the island's gastronomic heritage. The slow pace of life, inherent in Madeira's culture, encourages savoring each moment, each bite. Dining in family-owned restaurants, surrounded by the warmth of local hospitality, transforms meals into intimate experiences that linger in the memory.

Vibrant Festivals and Cultural Richness

Madeira is not just a destination; it is a celebration of life, color, and culture. Throughout the year, the island comes alive with vibrant festivals and events that reflect its rich heritage. The Carnival, with its elaborate parades and lively atmosphere, epitomizes the spirit of revelry. The Flower Festival, a symphony of colors, transforms the streets into a floral canvas. Participating in these celebrations allows visitors to not just witness but immerse themselves in the island's dynamic culture.

Adventure Beckons: Hiking, Water Sports, and Beyond

For those with an adventurous spirit, Madeira is an outdoor playground waiting to be explored. Hiking enthusiasts can navigate an extensive network of trails that reveal breathtaking panoramas, from mountain peaks to coastal cliffs. The surrounding Atlantic Ocean offers opportunities for whale watching, snorkeling, and diving, providing a unique perspective of the island's marine life. Whether it's conquering challenging peaks or embracing the tranquility of the sea, Madeira caters to the diverse desires of the intrepid traveler.

Warmth of Locals: A Genuine Welcome

Perhaps the most enduring allure of Madeira lies in the warmth of its people. As a traveler who values connections, the genuine welcome extended by locals adds an invaluable layer to the experience. Conversations in cafes, interactions in markets, and the shared laughter during festivals create a sense of belonging. In Madeira, every traveler is not just a visitor but a temporary member of a community that embraces and shares its treasures.

Capturing Moments, Creating Memories

Madeira is not just a destination; it's a collection of moments waiting to be captured and memories waiting to be made. Whether it's witnessing the sunrise from Pico do Arieiro, savoring a local delicacy in a hidden village, or dancing in the streets during a festival, each experience leaves an indelible mark on the traveler's soul. It's a place where time slows down, allowing for genuine connections and a deep appreciation of life's simple pleasures.

In essence, my fellow wanderers, Madeira is a destination that transcends the ordinary. It's an invitation to explore, to embrace, and to be captivated by the island's timeless beauty and genuine hospitality. As a veteran traveler, I extend a heartfelt invitation to embark on a journey that goes beyond the guidebooks and taps into the essence of Madeira – a place where every step is a discovery and every moment is an adventure. Let the island weave its magic, and may your sojourn in Madeira be an experience that lingers in your heart long after you bid it farewell.

WHAT TO EXPECT FROM THIS GUIDE

In the realm of travel, the allure of discovery is a beacon for wanderers, beckoning them to unearth the hidden gems of a destination. I present to you the **"Madeira Comprehensive Guide 2024 And Beyond"** – a meticulously crafted compendium that transcends the boundaries of conventional travel literature. This guide is not just a roadmap; it is an immersive journey into the heart and soul of Madeira, promising to unravel its secrets and invite you to explore its enchanting landscapes, rich culture, and vibrant communities.

Maps and Navigation: Charting Your Course

In the spirit of providing a holistic experience, the "Madeira Comprehensive Guide" is equipped with detailed maps and navigation aids. Navigating the island's intricate network of trails, coastal roads, and charming villages becomes a seamless endeavor. Whether you're an avid hiker or a leisurely explorer, these visual aids will guide you through the diverse landscapes with ease.

Accommodation Options: Your Home Away from Home

A traveler's sanctuary lies in the choice of accommodation. This guide leaves no stone unturned in presenting a diverse array of options – from luxury resorts in Funchal to quaint guest houses nestled in the rural hinterlands. Each recommendation is meticulously curated, ensuring that your stay in Madeira is not just comfortable but an integral part of the island's narrative.

Transportation: Navigating Madeira's Tapestry

Understanding the importance of seamless travel, this guide delves into the intricacies of transportation on the island. Whether you opt for the convenience of rental cars, the charm of local buses, or the efficiency of taxis, you'll find comprehensive information on getting around Madeira with ease.

Top Attractions: A Tapestry of Wonders

Madeira's allure lies in its myriad attractions, and this guide devotes ample space to unveil the island's top gems. From the iconic Pico do Arieiro to the historic charm of Funchal's Old Town, each attraction is intricately described, offering a glimpse into the diverse facets of Madeira's beauty.

Practical Information and Travel Resources: A Traveler's Handbook

A comprehensive guide is incomplete without practical information. From currency tips to language nuances, safety guidelines, and essential travel apps, this section ensures that you are armed with the knowledge needed for a seamless journey. A well-informed traveler is an empowered explorer.

Culinary Delights: A Feast for the Senses

The heart of any destination lies in its cuisine, and Madeira's gastronomic treasures are not to be missed. From traditional dishes like Espetada to the delectable sweetness of Madeira wine, the culinary section of this guide takes you on a sensory journey through the island's diverse and delicious offerings.

Culture and Heritage: Time-Travel Through Traditions

Immerse yourself in Madeira's rich culture and heritage with insights into its arts, crafts, historical sites, and traditional music. Uncover the island's soul through its cultural expressions, from the craftsmanship of local artisans to the captivating beats of traditional dance.

Outdoor Activities and Adventures: Where Nature Becomes Your Playground: For the adventurous soul, Madeira offers a wealth of outdoor activities. Explore hiking trails that unveil breathtaking vistas, engage in watersports along the coastline, and discover the island's natural beauty through a lens of adventure.

Shopping: Treasures to Take Home

Delve into the world of Madeiran shopping with a guide to local markets, specialty stores, and unique souvenirs. Whether you seek traditional crafts or contemporary designs, this guide directs you to the best shopping destinations on the island.

Day Trips and Excursions: Beyond the Horizon

Extend your exploration beyond the borders of Madeira with meticulously planned day trips. Uncover nearby islands, embark on scenic drives, and indulge in historical excursions that broaden your understanding of the archipelago's diversity.

Entertainment and Nightlife: Where the Island Comes Alive

As the sun sets, Madeira transforms into a vibrant tapestry of entertainment and nightlife. From cozy bars and pubs to energetic nightclubs, this guide navigates you through the nocturnal side of the island, ensuring your evenings are as enchanting as your days.

In conclusion, the "Madeira Comprehensive Guide" is more than just a manual; it's an invitation to embark on a journey of discovery. Through its pages, I aim to ignite your curiosity, inspire your wanderlust, and guide you through an immersive experience that transcends the ordinary. Madeira awaits, and within these pages, you'll find the keys to unlock its mysteries and treasures. So, let the adventure begin, and may the "Madeira Comprehensive Guide" be your trusted companion on this extraordinary voyage.

CHAPTER 1

INTRODUCTION TO MADEIRA

1.1 History and Heritage

The Discovery and Early Settlement:

The story of Madeira begins with its discovery in 1419 by Portuguese explorers João Gonçalves Zarco, Tristão Vaz Teixeira, and Bartolomeu Perestrelo. Legend has it that the island was named "Madeira" (meaning wood) due to the dense Laurissilva Forest that covered its terrain. The early settlers, mainly of Portuguese origin, carved out a life on this rugged land, cultivating crops and introducing sugarcane, which became a significant economic driver.

Sugarcane Era and Colonization:

The 15th and 16th centuries marked the sugarcane boom, transforming Madeira into a prosperous hub of sugarcane production. The island's fertile soil and favorable climate contributed to its economic success. However, the decline of the sugar industry led to a shift in focus towards viticulture, giving rise to the world-renowned Madeira wine.

Cultural Influences and Architectural Legacy:

Madeira's history is not confined to its economic pursuits; it is also imprinted in its architecture and cultural influences. The island's buildings, including churches, fortresses, and quintas (manor houses), bear witness to Portuguese, Moorish, and Gothic architectural styles. As you wander through Funchal's Old Town, the Sé Cathedral and São Tiago Fortress narrate tales of a bygone era.

Colonial Era and Foreign Influences:

During the Age of Exploration, Madeira served as a crucial stopover for navigators en route to the New World. The island's strategic location attracted attention from various powers, including Spain, England, and France. These influences left an indelible mark on Madeira's cultural mosaic, evident in its traditions, language, and even culinary delights.

Cultural Heritage and Traditions:

Madeira's cultural heritage is alive in its traditions, festivals, and folkloric expressions. The island's Fado music, a soul-stirring genre that tells tales of love, longing, and the sea, encapsulates the spirit of Madeiran culture. Festivals like the Carnival and the Flower Festival are vibrant showcases of local traditions, inviting visitors to partake in the island's joie de vivre.

Laurissilva Forest: A Living Relic:

One of the most remarkable aspects of Madeira's heritage is the Laurissilva Forest, a remnant of ancient laurel forest that once covered much of Southern Europe. Designated as a UNESCO World Heritage site, this lush greenery stands as a living relic, offering a glimpse into the island's prehistoric past.

Modern Era and Contemporary Resilience:

Madeira's history extends into the modern era, marked by periods of economic challenges and moments of resilience. The island has embraced tourism as a key industry, welcoming travelers to experience its unique blend of natural beauty and cultural charm.

Preserving the Past for the Future:

Efforts to preserve Madeira's history and heritage are evident in its museums, such as the Madeira Story Centre and the Museum of Sacred Art. These institutions serve as guardians of the island's past, showcasing artifacts, documents, and exhibits that tell the story of Madeira through the ages.

Practical Insights for Visitors:

For those keen on delving into Madeira's history, guided tours of historical sites, churches, and museums provide an immersive experience. The island's tourism infrastructure is designed to cater to history enthusiasts, offering a blend of exploration and education.

1.2 Geography and Climate

Geography: An Island Haven

Madeira, a volcanic archipelago, is composed of four main islands: Madeira, Porto Santo, and the uninhabited Desertas and Selvagens. The star of the show, Madeira Island, is a mountainous gem rising sharply from the ocean's depths. Picture steep cliffs, dramatic peaks, and deep valleys that form a rugged terrain, all blanketed by the lush greenery of the Laurissilva Forest – a UNESCO World Heritage site and a living relic from the Tertiary period.

Landscapes that Take Your Breath Away:

As you traverse the island, the diverse landscapes unfold before you. From the central mountain range crowned by Pico Ruivo, the highest peak, to the verdant hillsides covered in vineyards, every vista is a postcard-worthy moment. The Levadas, irrigation channels that crisscross the island, create a network of hiking trails that lead you through laurel forests, waterfalls, and panoramic viewpoints.

Coastal Beauty and Hidden Coves:

Madeira's coastline is a spectacle of contrasts. Steep cliffs plunge into the Atlantic, creating a dramatic backdrop to the cobalt-blue waters. Hidden coves and natural pools, such as the ones at Porto Moniz, invite visitors to embrace the sea. The coastal villages, with their colorful houses, are perched on the hillsides, offering a charming juxtaposition to the rugged landscapes.

Porto Santo: A Tranquil Oasis:

A short ferry ride away lies Porto Santo, a quieter sibling to Madeira. Known for its golden sandy beaches, Porto Santo offers a stark contrast to the volcanic terrain of Madeira. It's a haven for those seeking serenity, where azure waters meet pristine shores, providing an idyllic escape from the bustling world.

Climate: A Symphony of Seasons

Madeira's climate is a harmonious blend of subtropical and Mediterranean influences, creating a year-round haven for travelers. Winters are mild, and summers are warm without being sweltering, thanks to the moderating effect of the ocean. This unique climate fosters a lush, evergreen landscape and a kaleidoscope of blooming flowers that add bursts of color to the scenery.

The Trade Winds: Nature's Breath

The trade winds, gentle and consistent, sweep across the Atlantic, embracing Madeira in a caress that defines its climate. These winds moderate temperatures, create microclimates, and ensure a refreshing breeze that accompanies you on your explorations. The southern coast, shielded by the mountains, enjoys a warmer climate, while the north experiences a cooler and wetter atmosphere.

Rainfall and Microclimates:

Madeira's varied topography contributes to the creation of microclimates, each with its own charm. The northern slopes, kissed by moist air from the ocean, boast lush vegetation and frequent rainfall. In contrast, the southern slopes are drier, fostering vineyards and sun-soaked landscapes. The Laurissilva Forest, shrouded in mist, thrives in the central mountainous region.

Practical Insights for Visitors:

For those planning a visit, the climate ensures that there's never a wrong time to explore Madeira. Whether you choose the blooming spring, warm summer, colorful autumn, or the mild winter, the island offers a diverse range of experiences. Packing essentials include layers for varying temperatures, sturdy hiking shoes for trails, and swimwear for impromptu dips in natural pools.

1.3 Local Customs and Traditions

Fado: A Soulful Melody of Longing

In the atmospheric streets of Funchal and quaint village squares, the haunting notes of Fado resonate. This traditional Portuguese music, with its melancholic undertones and soulful lyrics, captures the essence of longing and saudade – a bittersweet yearning for something absent. Attend a Fado performance, and you'll find yourself transported to the emotional core of Madeira's cultural soul.

Carnival: A Riot of Color and Celebration

If there's a time when Madeira truly lets its hair down, it's during Carnival. This annual extravaganza is a vibrant display of colorful parades, flamboyant costumes, and infectious revelry. Join the locals in the lively processions, where streets pulse with energy and creativity. From intricately designed floats to masked dancers, Carnival is a celebration that transcends generations, uniting locals and visitors alike in joyous festivities.

Flower Festival: A Symphony of Petals

In spring, Madeira dons a floral mantle for the renowned Flower Festival. The streets burst into a riot of colors as flower-covered floats parade through Funchal. The air is infused with the sweet fragrance of blossoms, and locals adorn themselves in vibrant floral attire. It's a celebration of life, nature, and the island's horticultural richness that enchants every visitor lucky enough to witness this botanical spectacle.

Religious Celebrations: A Pious Affair

Religious traditions play a significant role in Madeiran life, and various festivals punctuate the calendar. The Feast of Corpus Christi transforms the streets into intricate floral carpets, a mesmerizing display of devotion and artistry. Pilgrimages to revered shrines, such as Nossa Senhora do Monte, offer insights into the islanders' deep-rooted spirituality and commitment to their religious heritage.

Madeiran Cuisine: A Feast of Tradition

To truly understand a culture, one must savor its culinary traditions. Madeiran cuisine is a delicious journey through local flavors and culinary customs. Espetada, a skewered meat delicacy, and the exotic passion fruit-infused dishes showcase the island's gastronomic heritage. Don't miss the opportunity to dine in a traditional Madeiran restaurant, where hearty meals are served with a side of warm hospitality.

Handcrafted Delights: Artisanal Heritage

Wander through local markets and artisan shops, and you'll discover the craftsmanship that defines Madeiran culture. Intricate lacework, known as "Madeira Embroidery," and wicker crafts are emblematic of the island's artisanal heritage. These handcrafted treasures not only make for unique souvenirs but also offer a glimpse into the skill and dedication of local craftsmen.

Fishing Traditions: A Maritime Legacy

Madeira's connection to the sea is deeply ingrained in its traditions. Fishing villages, like Camara de Lobos, exude a maritime charm that reflects the island's seafaring legacy. Join the locals at the fish market, where the day's catch is showcased in a bustling symphony of fishmongers and discerning buyers. It's a sensory experience that brings you closer to the island's maritime heartbeat.

Language and Social Etiquette: A Warm Welcome

The warmth of Madeiran hospitality is evident not just in the smiles but also in the language and social customs. While Portuguese is the official language, English is widely spoken, making communication easy for visitors. Politeness and friendliness are valued traits, and a simple "Bom dia" (Good morning) or "Obrigado" (Thank you) goes a long way in fostering connections with the locals.

Traditional Festivals: A Window into the Past

Throughout the year, Madeira hosts a myriad of traditional festivals that offer a glimpse into the island's past. The "Arraiais" (local festivities) are lively gatherings featuring folk music, traditional dances, and, of course, delicious local delicacies. Joining in these celebrations provides an authentic experience of Madeiran joy and community spirit.

Practical Insights for Visitors:

For those eager to engage in local customs, attending festivals and trying traditional foods are immersive ways to connect with Madeira's culture. Respectful participation in religious events and an openness to the warmth of local hospitality will undoubtedly enhance your stay on the island.

1.4 Madeira in the Present

Dynamic Funchal: The Heartbeat of Madeira

Funchal, the capital city, pulsates with life and energy, embodying the contemporary spirit of Madeira. Stroll through its bustling streets lined with shops, cafes, and vibrant markets. The Old Town, a maze of narrow alleys adorned with colorful doors and wrought-iron balconies, invites exploration. Cafes and restaurants spill onto cobbled squares, creating a lively atmosphere that captivates the senses.

Modern Infrastructure and Accessibility:

Madeira has embraced modernity without compromising its natural charm. The Cristiano Ronaldo International Airport, named after the football legend born in Funchal, ensures seamless connectivity for visitors. Well-maintained roads, public transportation options, and car rental services make exploring the island convenient. From luxury resorts to boutique accommodations, the island offers a range of options to suit every traveler's preference.

Contemporary Arts and Culture:

Beyond its historical treasures, Madeira is a hub of contemporary arts and culture. The Art Center Caravel and the Madeira Contemporary Art Museum showcase the works of local and international artists, reflecting the island's evolving cultural scene. The Teatro Municipal Baltazar Dias hosts theatrical performances, concerts, and events that contribute to Madeira's cultural dynamism.

Culinary Evolution: A Gastronomic Adventure

Madeira's culinary scene has evolved, offering a delightful fusion of traditional flavors and modern creativity. Trendy eateries in Funchal serve innovative dishes that highlight locally sourced ingredients. Explore the Rua de Santa Maria, where street art meets culinary innovation, creating an atmosphere that blends history with contemporary gastronomy.

Adventure Tourism and Outdoor Activities:

For the thrill-seekers, Madeira's present-day allure extends to adventure tourism. From hiking the challenging trails of Ponta de São Lourenço to engaging in water sports along the coastline, the island caters to adrenaline enthusiasts. Canyoning, paragliding, and mountain biking are just a few of the exhilarating activities awaiting those who seek an adventurous escape.

Sustainable Tourism Initiatives:

Madeira is committed to preserving its natural beauty, evident in its sustainable tourism initiatives. The Laurissilva Forest, a UNESCO World Heritage site, is protected, and eco-friendly practices are encouraged. Visitors can participate in nature conservation programs and support local businesses committed to environmentally conscious practices.

Festivals and Events: A Year-Round Celebration

Madeira's calendar is adorned with festivals and events throughout the year. From the lively Carnival and Flower Festival to the Madeira Wine Festival, visitors can partake in the island's joyous celebrations. The Christmas and New Year festivities, marked by dazzling lights and fireworks, transform Funchal into a winter wonderland, attracting visitors from around the world.

Digital Nomad Haven: Remote Work in Paradise

In tune with global trends, Madeira has become an appealing destination for digital nomads seeking a picturesque backdrop for remote work. With reliable internet connectivity, co-working spaces, and the allure of the island's natural beauty, Madeira offers a tranquil escape for those looking to balance work and leisure.

Practical Insights for Visitors

As you plan your visit to Madeira, consider the island's diverse offerings. Pack accordingly for both urban exploration and outdoor adventures. Familiarize yourself with the local customs, indulge in contemporary culinary delights, and embrace the island's dynamic spirit.

1.5 Getting to Know the Locals

Beyond the breathtaking landscapes and vibrant festivals, the true essence of Madeira lies in the warmth and authenticity of its people. As you embark on your journey to this Atlantic haven, the opportunity to connect with the locals becomes a tapestry of meaningful experiences. Join me as we explore the art of getting to know the heart of Madeira – its locals – and discover the genuine warmth that awaits every visitor.

The Warm Greetings: A Cultural Embrace

From the moment you set foot on Madeiran soil, expect to be enveloped in genuine warmth. Locals extend heartfelt greetings, often accompanied by a welcoming smile. The traditional Portuguese saying, "Bem-vindo!" meaning "Welcome!" echoes through the streets and shops, setting the tone for the hospitality that defines Madeira.

Cafés and Local Hangouts: A Window to Daily Life

For an authentic taste of Madeiran life, linger in local cafés and popular hangouts. Join the rhythmic conversations as locals gather to discuss daily affairs, share stories, and savor the island's renowned coffee. Café culture is not just about the brew; it's a social experience that provides a glimpse into the heart of Madeira's community spirit.

Markets and Street Vendors: Connecting through Commerce

Exploring the bustling markets, such as the Mercado dos Lavradores in Funchal, offers more than just a shopping experience. Engage with friendly vendors, sample local produce, and let the vibrant colors of fruits, flowers, and crafts be a catalyst for spontaneous conversations. It's a chance to connect with locals who take pride in their offerings and are eager to share their stories.

Festivals and Celebrations: Shared Joy and Camaraderie

Madeira's festivals are not just spectacles for visitors; they are invitations to become part of the local tapestry. Joining in the revelry of Carnival, dancing in the streets during the Flower Festival, or participating in the Arraiais (local festivities) during summer provides opportunities to share joy and camaraderie with the islanders.

Participate in Local Traditions: A Cultural Immersion

Immerse yourself in Madeira's rich cultural traditions by participating in local activities. Attend a Fado performance, learn traditional dance steps, or try your hand at making Espetada, the iconic skewered meat dish. The locals appreciate visitors who show an interest in their customs, creating moments of cultural exchange and shared experiences.

Laurissilva Forest: Nature's Classroom with Locals

Venture into the Laurissilva Forest, a UNESCO World Heritage site, and let locals guide you through this natural wonder. Many islanders are passionate about preserving their environment, and joining guided nature walks or conservation activities provides a unique opportunity to bond over a shared love for the island's flora and fauna.

Small Village Exploration: Hidden Gems of Hospitality

Beyond the capital, Funchal, explore the small villages where the heartbeat of Madeira is most palpable. In places like Santana or Ponta do Sol, locals welcome visitors with open arms. Engage in conversations, visit local taverns, and experience the unhurried pace of village life, where genuine hospitality thrives.

Language and Communication: A Friendly Bridge

While Portuguese is the official language, English is widely spoken, especially in tourist areas. However, attempting a few Portuguese phrases, like "Bom dia" (Good morning) or "Obrigado" (Thank you), is appreciated and often met with smiles. The locals value the effort to bridge linguistic gaps and are eager to assist visitors in navigating their way through the island.

Social Etiquette: Embracing Local Customs

Understanding social etiquette is key to fostering connections in Madeira. Politeness, respect for personal space, and a genuine interest in local customs go a long way. If invited into someone's home, it's customary to bring a small gift as a token of appreciation. Such gestures contribute to building meaningful connections and friendships.

Practical Insights for Visitors:

Approaching interactions with an open heart and a genuine curiosity about Madeiran life will undoubtedly enhance your experience. Respect local customs, be receptive to invitations, and consider participating in community activities for a more immersive stay.

In concluding this exploration of getting to know the locals in Madeira, envision a journey enriched by shared stories and lasting bonds. The island's true magic lies not just in its landscapes but in the welcoming embrace of its people. As you connect with locals and become a temporary part of their world, may you find that the heart of Madeira beats not only in its natural wonders but in the genuine and friendly spirit of its inhabitants. Embrace the opportunity to forge connections that transcend borders and make your visit to Madeira a journey of shared joy and cultural enrichment.

CHAPTER 2

ACCOMMODATION OPTIONS

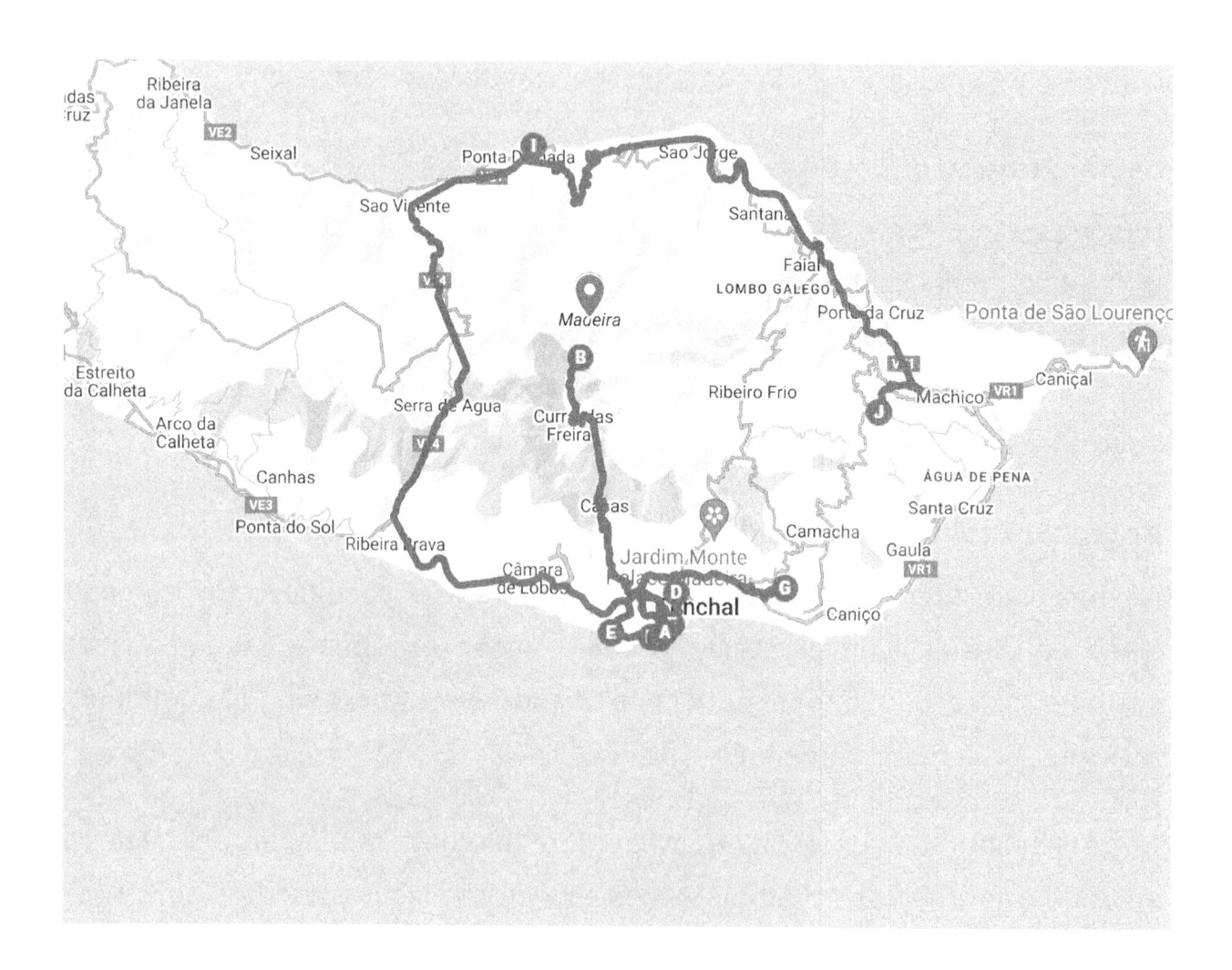

2.1 Hotels and Resorts

Belmond Reid's Palace:

Perched on the cliffside overlooking the Atlantic Ocean, Belmond Reid's Palace stands as an epitome of timeless elegance. Located in the capital city of Funchal, this iconic hotel has been a symbol of luxury since 1891. With its colonial charm, the property boasts meticulously manicured gardens, opulent rooms with ocean views, and exceptional service. Prices for lodging range from €300 to €1500 per night, depending on the room type and season. Guests can indulge in a range of amenities, including a spa, fine dining restaurants, and a private beach area. The unique feature of Belmond Reid's Palace is the afternoon tea served on the terrace, allowing guests to savor delectable treats while soaking in panoramic vistas.

The Cliff Bay:

Situated in the picturesque area of Funchal Bay, The Cliff Bay is a five-star hotel renowned for its contemporary design and breathtaking views. Prices for accommodation at The Cliff Bay start at €250 and can go up to €1200 per night. The hotel's amenities include a seawater pool, a Michelin-starred restaurant, and a wellness center. The unique feature of this establishment is its access to a private sea platform, providing guests with an exclusive opportunity to enjoy the crystal-clear waters of the Atlantic.

Quinta Jardins do Lago:

For those seeking a tranquil escape, Quinta Jardins do Lago is a hidden gem nestled in the heart of Funchal. Surrounded by lush botanical gardens, this boutique hotel offers an oasis of serenity. Prices for lodging range from €200 to €800 per night. The hotel features a spacious swimming pool, a spa, and an acclaimed restaurant serving Madeiran and international cuisine. The unique feature of Quinta Jardins do Lago lies in its 18th-century manor house, providing guests with a glimpse into the island's history and culture.

Pestana Royal Premium All-Inclusive Ocean & Spa Resort:

Located on the west coast of Madeira in the vibrant town of Funchal, the Pestana Royal Premium All-Inclusive Ocean & Spa Resort is a haven for those seeking an all-encompassing holiday experience. Prices for accommodation start at €180 and can go up to €900 per night. The resort offers a variety of amenities, including multiple swimming pools, a spa, and a range of restaurants. The unique feature of Pestana Royal is its all-inclusive concept, allowing guests to enjoy a diverse culinary experience and a wide array of activities without worrying about additional costs.

Savoy Palace:

Rising majestically in the heart of Funchal, the Savoy Palace is a symbol of modern luxury and sophistication. With its contemporary architecture and panoramic views of the city and sea, this five-star hotel is a magnet for discerning travelers. Prices for lodging at the Savoy Palace start at €300 and can reach up to €2000 per night for premium suites. The hotel boasts a rooftop infinity pool, a spa, and several dining options. The unique feature of Savoy Palace is its avant-garde design, seamlessly blending modernity with the island's natural beauty.

Casa Velha do Palheiro:

Away from the bustling city life, Casa Velha do Palheiro is an intimate boutique hotel nestled within the Palheiro Gardens estate. Located in the hills above Funchal, the hotel provides a peaceful retreat surrounded by lush greenery. Prices for accommodation range from €180 to €800 per night. The hotel offers a golf course, a spa, and a restaurant serving traditional Madeiran cuisine. The unique feature of Casa Velha do Palheiro is its proximity to the Palheiro Gardens, allowing guests to explore the diverse flora and fauna of Madeira at their leisure.

Madeira's hotels and resorts offer a diverse range of experiences, from the historic elegance of Belmond Reid's Palace to the modern luxury of Savoy Palace. Whether seeking tranquility, adventure, or a blend of both, these accommodations cater to the diverse preferences of visitors. With each establishment contributing its unique charm, Madeira stands as a destination where the beauty of the landscape is complemented by the comfort and hospitality of its exceptional hotels and resorts.

2.2 Guesthouses and Bed & Breakfasts

Vila Vicência:

Nestled in the quaint village of Ponta do Sol, Vila Vicência is a charming guesthouse that captures the essence of Madeiran hospitality. With prices ranging from €70 to €150 per night, it offers budget-friendly accommodation without compromising on comfort. The guesthouse features cozy rooms with traditional décor, a communal kitchen for guests, and a garden terrace with panoramic views of the ocean. The unique feature of Vila Vicência is its emphasis on a personalized experience, where the hosts go the extra mile to make guests feel like they are staying in a home away from home.

Casa da Capelinha:

Tucked away in the scenic hills of São Vicente, Casa da Capelinha is a picturesque bed & breakfast surrounded by lush landscapes. Prices for lodging range from €90 to €200 per night. The rooms, adorned with rustic charm, offer a peaceful retreat. The amenities include a swimming pool, a terrace with sweeping views, and a restaurant serving authentic Madeiran cuisine. The unique feature of Casa da Capelinha is its location amidst vineyards and mountains, providing guests with a serene escape from the bustling city life.

Estalagem a Quinta:

In the heart of Ponta do Pargo, Estalagem a Quinta is a tranquil guesthouse that beckons travelers seeking a peaceful refuge. Prices for accommodation start at €80 and can go up to €160 per night. The guesthouse features spacious rooms with traditional furnishings, a garden with a swimming pool, and a restaurant offering locally sourced ingredients. The unique feature of Estalagem a Quinta is its proximity to Ponta do Pargo Lighthouse, allowing guests to explore the westernmost point of Madeira easily.

Casa das Videiras:

Located in the historic center of Funchal, Casa das Videiras is a charming bed & breakfast housed in a restored 18th-century building. Prices for lodging range from €100 to €180 per night. The B&B offers elegantly decorated rooms, a courtyard garden, and a communal lounge area. The unique feature of Casa das Videiras is its historical significance, allowing guests to experience the architectural heritage of Madeira while enjoying modern comforts.

Casa do Velho Dragoeiro:

In the coastal town of Machico, Casa do Velho Dragoeiro is a delightful bed & breakfast that combines comfort with proximity to the island's natural beauty. Prices for accommodation start at €80 and can go up to €150 per night. The guesthouse features cozy rooms with sea views, a communal kitchen, and a terrace. The unique feature of Casa do Velho Dragoeiro is its close proximity to Machico Beach, providing guests with easy access to one of Madeira's stunning sandy shores.

Solar da Bica:

Perched on a hillside in Ribeira Brava, Solar da Bica is a charming guesthouse that offers panoramic views of the surrounding mountains and ocean. Prices for lodging range from €70 to €140 per night. The guesthouse features comfortable rooms with traditional décor, a garden with a swimming pool, and a terrace for relaxation. The unique feature of Solar da Bica is its emphasis on sustainability, incorporating eco-friendly practices to ensure a responsible and immersive experience for guests.

While grand hotels define luxury, Madeira's guesthouses and bed & breakfasts carve a niche for themselves by offering a more intimate and authentic connection to the island. From the historic charm of Casa das Videiras to the serene retreat of Estalagem a Quinta, each establishment invites visitors to experience the warmth and hospitality that define Madeira's unique allure.

2.3 Vacation Rentals

Casa do Lugarinho:

Nestled in the hills of São Vicente, Casa do Lugarinho offers a tranquil escape surrounded by lush greenery. Prices for lodging range from €80 to €150 per night, making it an attractive option for those seeking budget-friendly yet comfortable accommodation. The vacation rental features fully equipped apartments with private balconies, a shared garden, and barbecue facilities. The unique feature of Casa do Lugarinho is its proximity to São Vicente Caves and Volcanism Center, allowing guests easy access to geological wonders.

Villa Albatroz:

Perched on the cliffs of Ponta do Sol, Villa Albatroz is a stunning vacation rental offering breathtaking views of the Atlantic Ocean. Prices for accommodation start at €120 and can go up to €300 per night. The villa includes spacious living areas, a private swimming pool, and a terrace for al fresco dining. The unique feature of Villa Albatroz is its direct access to the ocean through a private pathway, providing guests with an exclusive opportunity to enjoy the sea.

Casa do Penhasco:

Situated in the charming village of Arco de São Jorge, Casa do Penhasco is a cozy vacation rental surrounded by vineyards and mountains. Prices for lodging range from €70 to €120 per night, offering affordable accommodation with a touch of rustic charm. The rental includes self-catering cottages with kitchen facilities, a garden, and a terrace with panoramic views. The unique feature of Casa do Penhasco is its proximity to the Levada do Rei hiking trail, inviting nature enthusiasts to explore the island's scenic landscapes.

Casa da Eira:

Located in the heart of Santana, Casa da Eira is a traditional vacation rental set amidst the picturesque landscapes of the Madeiran countryside. Prices for accommodation start at €90 and can go up to €180 per night. The rental comprises cozy cottages with wooden interiors, a garden, and a barbecue area. The unique feature of Casa da Eira is its location near the famous Santana thatched houses and the Madeira Theme Park, allowing guests to delve into the island's culture and history.

Villa Paraiso:

Overlooking the bay of Funchal, Villa Paraiso is a luxurious vacation rental offering a private oasis in the bustling city. Prices for lodging range from €200 to €500 per night, catering to those seeking a lavish retreat. The villa boasts spacious living areas, a private swimming pool, and a terrace with panoramic views. The unique feature of Villa Paraiso is its proximity to the city center, allowing guests to explore Funchal's vibrant culture, restaurants, and nightlife with ease.

Quinta das Vinhas:

In the wine-producing region of Estreito de Câmara de Lobos, Quinta das Vinhas is a charming vacation rental surrounded by vineyards and mountains. Prices for accommodation range from €100 to €200 per night. The rental features self-catering cottages with private balconies, a shared swimming pool, and a garden. The unique feature of Quinta das Vinhas is its wine-producing heritage, offering guests the opportunity to savor local wines while enjoying the tranquility of the countryside.

2.4 Camping Sites

Parque de Campismo Porto Moniz:

Nestled on the northwest coast, Parque de Campismo Porto Moniz offers a stunning seaside camping experience. Prices for lodging range from €10 to €20 per night, making it an affordable choice for budget-conscious travelers. The camping site provides basic facilities such as toilets, showers, and a communal kitchen. The unique feature of Parque de Campismo Porto Moniz is its proximity to the natural pools of Porto Moniz, inviting campers to take a refreshing dip in the Atlantic while surrounded by volcanic rocks.

Parque de Campismo Pico da Areia:

Situated in the heart of the Laurissilva Forest, Parque de Campismo Pico da Areia provides a secluded camping experience immersed in nature. Prices for accommodation start at €15 and can go up to €30 per night. The camping site offers basic amenities, including toilets and showers, allowing campers to enjoy a rustic yet comfortable stay. The unique feature of Parque de Campismo Pico da Areia is its access to hiking trails, providing campers with the opportunity to explore the ancient laurel forest and its diverse flora and fauna.

Parque de Campismo Madalena do Mar:

Perched on the cliffs overlooking the Atlantic, Parque de Campismo Madalena do Mar offers a breathtaking camping location with panoramic ocean views. Prices for lodging range from €12 to €25 per night, providing an affordable option for those seeking a coastal camping experience. The site offers essential facilities such as toilets, showers, and a communal kitchen. The unique feature of Parque de Campismo Madalena do Mar is its proximity to the scenic village of Jardim do Mar, allowing campers to explore the charming streets and enjoy local cuisine.

Parque de Campismo Faja da Ovelha:

In the tranquil village of Faja da Ovelha, this camping site provides a serene escape on the southwestern coast of Madeira. Prices for accommodation start at €10 and can go up to €20 per night, making it an economical choice for campers. The site offers basic amenities, including toilets and showers, in a peaceful rural setting. The unique feature of Parque de Campismo Faja da Ovelha is its location near Ponta do Pargo, allowing campers to witness the mesmerizing sunset at the westernmost point of the island.

Parque de Campismo Ribeira Funda:

Located in the lush Ribeira Funda Valley, this camping site offers a secluded retreat surrounded by mountains and waterfalls. Prices for lodging range from €15 to €30 per night, providing an affordable option for those seeking a nature-centric camping experience. The site provides basic facilities, allowing campers to immerse themselves in the tranquility of the valley. The unique feature of Parque de Campismo Ribeira Funda is its access to hiking trails leading to the impressive Risco Waterfall, offering a picturesque backdrop for camping enthusiasts.

Madeira's camping sites provide a gateway to the island's natural beauty, allowing visitors to sleep under the stars and wake up to the sounds of nature. From seaside vistas at Parque de Campismo Porto Moniz to the secluded forests of Parque de Campismo Pico da Areia, each camping site offers a distinctive experience for those eager to embrace the rugged charm of Madeira's outdoors.

2.5 Unique Stays and Boutique Hotels

Quinta do Furão:

Nestled in the northeastern part of Madeira, Quinta do Furão is a charming boutique hotel set amidst terraced vineyards overlooking the Atlantic Ocean. Prices for lodging range from €120 to €300 per night. The hotel features well-appointed rooms, a swimming pool with panoramic views, and a renowned restaurant offering Madeiran and international cuisine. The unique feature of Quinta do Furão is its wine cellar, allowing guests to savor the region's exquisite wines while enjoying the tranquility of the surrounding countryside.

Castanheiro Boutique Hotel:

Situated in the heart of Funchal's historic center, Castanheiro Boutique Hotel is a blend of old-world charm and modern luxury. Prices for accommodation start at €150 and can go up to €400 per night. The hotel boasts elegantly designed rooms, a rooftop terrace with a pool, and a spa. The unique feature of Castanheiro Boutique Hotel is its location within a restored 18th-century building, preserving the architectural heritage of Funchal while providing guests with a sophisticated and comfortable retreat.

Saccharum Resort & Spa:

Located in Calheta on the southwest coast, Saccharum Resort & Spa is a contemporary design hotel that harmoniously blends with the surrounding landscapes. Prices for lodging range from €180 to €500 per night. The hotel offers spacious rooms with ocean views, multiple swimming pools, and a spa. The unique feature of Saccharum Resort & Spa is its integration with the sugar cane mill, providing guests with a glimpse into Madeira's agricultural history.

Quinta das Vistas Palace Gardens:

Perched on a hillside overlooking Funchal, Quinta das Vistas Palace Gardens is a luxurious boutique hotel surrounded by lush gardens. Prices for accommodation start at €200 and can reach up to €600 per night. The hotel features opulent rooms, a terrace with panoramic views, and a gourmet restaurant. The unique feature of Quinta das Vistas is its extensive botanical gardens, allowing guests to wander through a variety of exotic plants and flowers while enjoying the serenity of the property.

Casa do Miradouro:

Situated in the charming village of Ponta do Sol, Casa do Miradouro is a boutique guesthouse that offers a blend of authenticity and comfort. Prices for lodging range from €100 to €250 per night. The guesthouse features uniquely decorated rooms, a terrace with sea views, and a communal kitchen. The unique feature of Casa do Miradouro is its emphasis on local experiences, offering guests the opportunity to participate in traditional Madeiran cooking classes and cultural events.

Quinta do Riacho:

In the rural village of Santo da Serra, Quinta do Riacho is a boutique accommodation that provides an idyllic escape into nature. Prices for accommodation range from €80 to €180 per night. The property offers cozy rooms, a garden with walking trails, and a restaurant serving locally inspired dishes. The unique feature of Quinta do Riacho is its proximity to Santo da Serra Golf Course, allowing guests to combine a relaxing stay with a round of golf in the picturesque surroundings.

CHAPTER 3

TRANSPORTATION IN MADEIRA

3.1 Getting to Madeira

Air Travel

The primary mode of accessing Madeira is through air travel. The Madeira Airport, officially known as Cristiano Ronaldo International Airport, serves as the main point of entry. Numerous airlines connect Madeira to major European cities, providing travelers with convenient options. The cost of flying to Madeira can vary based on factors such as departure location, time of booking, and travel season. On average, a round-trip ticket from major European cities can range from €150 to €400. It is advisable to book in advance to secure the best fares. Several airlines operate direct flights to

Madeira, including TAP Air Portugal, easyJet, and British Airways. These carriers offer regular services from major European hubs like Lisbon, London, and Frankfurt.

Sea Routes

For those who prefer a scenic sea voyage, ferry services and cruise ships are available. However, sea travel to Madeira is not as common as air travel and requires careful planning.

Ferries

Ferries from Portugal's mainland, particularly from Lisbon and Portimão, offer an alternative means of reaching Madeira. The journey, while longer than by air, provides a unique perspective of the Atlantic coastline. Costs for ferry travel typically range from €50 to €100, depending on the chosen route.

Cruise Ships

Cruise enthusiasts can embark on a maritime adventure to Madeira by selecting cruise itineraries that include the island. Cruise costs vary significantly based on factors like cruise line, cabin type, and duration. Prices typically start at €500 and can go up to several thousand euros.

Land Travel

For those already in Portugal or nearby regions, driving to Madeira is an option. The island is accessible by car via the "Via Expresso," a highway network that connects various parts of Madeira. Travelers can rent a car from major cities like Funchal and explore the island's picturesque landscapes at their own pace. Rental costs range from €30 to €80 per day, depending on the vehicle type and rental duration.

Logistics and Practical Tips

Visa Requirements

Before embarking on the journey to Madeira, ensure compliance with visa requirements. European Union citizens typically do not need a visa for short stays, but it is crucial to check and plan accordingly for non-EU travelers.

Currency and Banking

Madeira uses the Euro (€) as its official currency. ATMs are widely available, and credit cards are accepted in most establishments. It is advisable to inform your bank about your travel dates to avoid any issues with card transactions.

Weather Considerations

Madeira enjoys a mild climate throughout the year, making it an attractive destination. However, travelers should be aware of occasional rain and variable weather conditions, especially during the winter months.

3.2 Public Transportation

Funchal's Bus System

The backbone of public transportation in Madeira is undoubtedly the bus system in Funchal, the capital city. Operated by Horários do Funchal, these buses connect different parts of Funchal and extend to various destinations across the island. The cost for a single journey typically ranges from €1.95 to €3.35, depending on the distance traveled. Bus stops are strategically positioned throughout Funchal, including Avenida do Mar, Praça do Município, and the Funchal Ecological Park.

Rodoeste - Regional Bus Services

Beyond Funchal, Rodoeste provides regional bus services, connecting towns and villages across Madeira. The cost varies based on the distance covered, with fares ranging from €2.50 to €8.00. Major stations include the Funchal Central Bus Station, where travelers can find routes to destinations like Câmara de Lobos and Machico.

Cable Car

For a unique transportation experience with unparalleled views, the Funchal Cable Car offers a breathtaking journey from the city to the hilltop parish of Monte. Priced at €16.00 for a round trip, the cable car provides an immersive perspective of Madeira's lush landscapes and the vast expanse of the Atlantic. Stations can be found near the Old Town in Funchal, allowing easy access for tourists and locals alike.

Aerobus - Connecting Airport to City

Facilitating seamless airport transfers, the Aerobus service connects Madeira Airport to various locations in Funchal. With a fare of €5.00 per person, this convenient mode of transportation ensures hassle-free travel for arriving and departing passengers. Stations include the airport terminal and key points in Funchal such as Avenida do Mar and Praia Formosa.

Taxis and Shared Taxis

While not a traditional public transportation mode, taxis play a crucial role in Madeira's mobility. Taxis operate on a metered system, with initial fares starting at €4.00 and additional charges based on distance. Additionally, shared taxis, known as "aluguer," provide a cost-effective option for commuting between towns, with fixed fares depending on the destination.

Renting a Car

For those seeking autonomy in their exploration of Madeira, renting a car becomes an appealing option. Rental costs vary depending on the vehicle type and rental duration, starting at approximately €30.00 per day. Numerous car rental agencies operate in Funchal, including options at Madeira Airport, providing convenient access for travelers.

Coastal Transportation: Ferries and Catamarans

Madeira's coastal geography makes maritime transportation a noteworthy option. Ferries and catamarans connect Funchal to Porto Santo, offering a scenic journey across the Atlantic. Prices range from €25.00 to €50.00 for a round trip, and the journey takes approximately 2 hours. Departures occur from the Funchal Marina, providing a memorable experience for those exploring the archipelago.

Walking Trails and Levadas

For nature enthusiasts, exploring Madeira's extensive network of walking trails and levadas (irrigation channels turned hiking paths) offers a unique way to traverse the island. While not conventional public transportation, these paths provide an eco-friendly and immersive means of experiencing Madeira's diverse landscapes.

3.3 Car Rentals and Driving Tips

Car Rental Locations in Madeira

Madeira boasts several car rental agencies, conveniently located at key points across the island. The main international airport, Cristiano Ronaldo Madeira International Airport, serves as a hub for car rental services. Leading rental companies, including Avis, Hertz, and Europcar, have counters within the airport premises, providing travelers with easy access to rental services upon arrival. In addition to the airport, Funchal, the capital city, is dotted with various car rental offices. The downtown area and major hotels often house branches of well-known rental agencies, giving visitors the flexibility to choose a location that suits their convenience. Exploring options online or contacting the agencies directly can help secure the best deals and availability.

Cost of Car Rentals in Madeira

The cost of renting a car in Madeira varies depending on factors such as the type of vehicle, rental duration, and the season. On average, small economy cars can be rented for around €30 to €50 per day, while larger SUVs or premium vehicles may cost between €60 and €100 per day. Special discounts and offers are often available for longer rental periods, providing cost-effective solutions for those planning extended stays. It's important to note that prices can fluctuate based on demand, so booking in advance is advisable for securing competitive rates. Additionally, travelers should factor in additional costs such as fuel, insurance, and potential tolls when budgeting for their car rental adventure.

Duration of Car Rentals

Car rental durations in Madeira are flexible to accommodate varying travel itineraries. Most agencies offer options ranging from daily rentals to weekly or even monthly arrangements. Short-term rentals are popular among tourists exploring the island for a few days, while long-term options appeal to those seeking an extended exploration. Daily rates are commonly available and may include unlimited mileage, providing the freedom to cover significant distances without incurring additional charges. Weekly rentals often come with discounted rates, making them cost-effective for travelers planning a more leisurely exploration of Madeira.

Driving Tips for Navigating Madeira's Roads

Madeira's roads offer a scenic journey through lush landscapes, but they can be challenging for those unfamiliar with the terrain. Here are some driving tips to ensure a safe and enjoyable experience:

Mountainous Terrain Awareness: Madeira is characterized by mountainous terrain with winding roads. Exercise caution, especially when navigating the steep inclines and declines. Be prepared for narrow roads, and always yield to oncoming traffic when the road narrows.

Explore Coastal Roads: Some of Madeira's most breathtaking views can be experienced along its coastal roads. Drive along the Estrada Monumental for stunning vistas of the Atlantic Ocean and the rugged coastline. Keep in mind that these routes may have sharp turns and elevation changes.

Weather Conditions: Madeira's weather can be unpredictable, with sudden rain or fog. Drive with caution in adverse weather conditions, and consider renting a car with good traction and stability features.

Parking in Funchal: In the bustling capital of Funchal, parking can be challenging. Opt for accommodations with parking facilities or utilize public parking areas. Exploring the city on foot or using public transportation may be a practical choice to avoid parking woes.

Tunnels and Bridges: Madeira features a network of tunnels and impressive bridges. Exercise patience and adhere to speed limits when navigating these structures. Use headlights in tunnels for safety and visibility.

3.4 Taxis and Ride-Sharing

Taxi Services in Madeira

Taxis are readily available throughout Madeira, offering a convenient and efficient means of transportation. Taxis can be hailed on the street or found at designated taxi stands in popular areas. The cost of a taxi ride in Madeira is influenced by factors such as distance, time of day, and the number of passengers. The base fare for a taxi in Madeira typically starts around €3 to €4, with an additional charge per kilometer, ranging from €0.50 to €1.00. It's important to note that prices may vary slightly among different taxi companies. Taxis can be a viable option for short distances or when traveling with luggage, providing a door-to-door service that is both comfortable and reliable.

Ride-Sharing Services in Madeira

In recent years, ride-sharing services have gained popularity worldwide, offering an alternative to traditional taxis. Madeira has embraced this trend, and several ride-sharing platforms operate on the island, providing users with a convenient way to request rides through mobile applications. Popular ride-sharing apps such as Uber and Bolt are available in Madeira, allowing users to book rides with ease. The cost of a ride-sharing journey is calculated based on factors similar to traditional taxis, including distance and time. The competitive pricing of ride-sharing services often makes them an attractive option for budget-conscious travelers.

Cost Comparison: Taxis vs. Ride-Sharing

Comparing the costs of taxis and ride-sharing services can help travelers make informed decisions based on their preferences and budget. While taxi fares are regulated and may have a standardized structure, ride-sharing prices can fluctuate based on demand and other factors. On average, the cost per kilometer for ride-sharing services in Madeira is comparable to that of traditional taxis. However, ride-sharing platforms may offer promotions, discounts, or surge pricing during peak hours, impacting the overall cost. Travelers should consider these variables when choosing between taxis and ride-sharing for their transportation needs.

Availability and Coverage

Taxis are widely available in popular tourist areas, main cities, and at transportation hubs such as airports and bus stations. However, in more remote or less frequented locations, taxi availability may be limited, and advance booking might be advisable. Ride-sharing services, on the other hand, leverage their app-based model to cover a broader geographic area. Users can request rides from almost anywhere on the island, making ride-sharing a versatile option for those exploring off-the-beaten-path destinations.

Booking Taxis and Ride-Shares

To book a taxi in Madeira, one can either hail one on the street or visit a designated taxi stand. Additionally, most taxi companies offer phone booking services, allowing users to schedule a pick-up at a specific time and location. For ride-sharing services, users need to download the respective app, create an account, and enter their payment information. The app allows users to input their desired pick-up and drop-off locations, providing an estimated fare before confirming the ride. This streamlined process enhances the overall convenience of ride-sharing in Madeira.

Regulations and Safety

Taxis in Madeira are subject to local regulations, ensuring that drivers adhere to established standards of safety and service. Licensed taxi drivers undergo background checks, and their vehicles are regularly inspected to maintain a high level of safety for passengers. Ride-sharing services also implement safety measures, including background checks for drivers and a system for users to rate their experiences. However, travelers should exercise caution and verify that the ride-sharing platform they choose complies with local regulations to ensure a secure and reliable journey.

3.5 Navigating Madeira's Roads

Road Network Overview

Madeira's road network is well-developed, connecting the main towns and providing access to stunning landscapes. The primary highways, such as the VR1 and VR2, link Funchal, the capital, to key destinations. While these roads offer swift travel, the real allure lies in the secondary roads that unveil hidden gems. Expect narrow, winding roads that meander through lush greenery and reveal breathtaking vistas.

Driving Regulations

Before embarking on your Madeira road adventure, familiarize yourself with Portuguese driving regulations. Drive on the right side of the road, adhere to speed limits (typically 50-90 km/h on rural roads), and always wear seat belts. Be cautious on sharp bends, and keep an eye out for local wildlife, especially in rural areas.

Renting a Vehicle

To fully explore Madeira's diverse landscapes, renting a vehicle is advisable. Car rental agencies are present at the airport and in major towns. Choose a vehicle that suits the terrain; smaller cars are ideal for navigating narrow roads, while more robust options may be preferred for mountainous regions.

Mountain Roads and Tunnels

Madeira's dramatic topography means you'll encounter mountainous terrain and intricate tunnel systems. The ER101, known as the Encumeada Road, leads through the mountains, offering spectacular views. While the tunnels facilitate travel through the rugged landscape, be prepared for varying light conditions and have your headlights on when driving through them.

Coastal Roads and Scenic Routes

For a captivating coastal drive, explore the roads along Madeira's rugged coastline. The ER101 and ER222 provide stunning ocean views, with opportunities to stop at viewpoints like Cabo Girão, one of the highest sea cliffs globally. Embrace the journey and take breaks to absorb the breathtaking scenery.

Weather and Road Conditions

Madeira's climate is mild, but weather conditions can change rapidly, especially in mountainous regions. Check weather forecasts before your journey and be prepared for rain, especially during the winter months. Rain may affect road conditions, so drive cautiously, particularly on steep slopes.

Parking in Towns and Villages

Navigating Madeira's charming towns and villages involves understanding parking nuances. Most towns have designated parking areas, and some may require payment. Plan your visit during non-peak hours to secure parking spaces easily. In Funchal, consider using public transportation or walking due to narrow streets and limited parking.

GPS Navigation and Offline Maps

Ensure a smooth journey by using a reliable GPS navigation system or mobile maps application. While major roads are well-marked, secondary routes may require navigation assistance. Download offline maps to avoid connectivity issues, especially in remote areas.

Local Driving Etiquette

Respect local driving etiquette to ensure a harmonious travel experience. Be patient on narrow roads, yielding to oncoming traffic when necessary. Honk your horn on blind curves to signal your presence. Embrace the unhurried pace of Madeiran driving culture.

Emergency Contacts and Services

Prioritize safety by keeping emergency contacts and services readily available. The emergency number in Portugal is 112. Familiarize yourself with local hospitals, service stations, and police stations along your route.

CHAPTER 4

TOP ATTRACTIONS

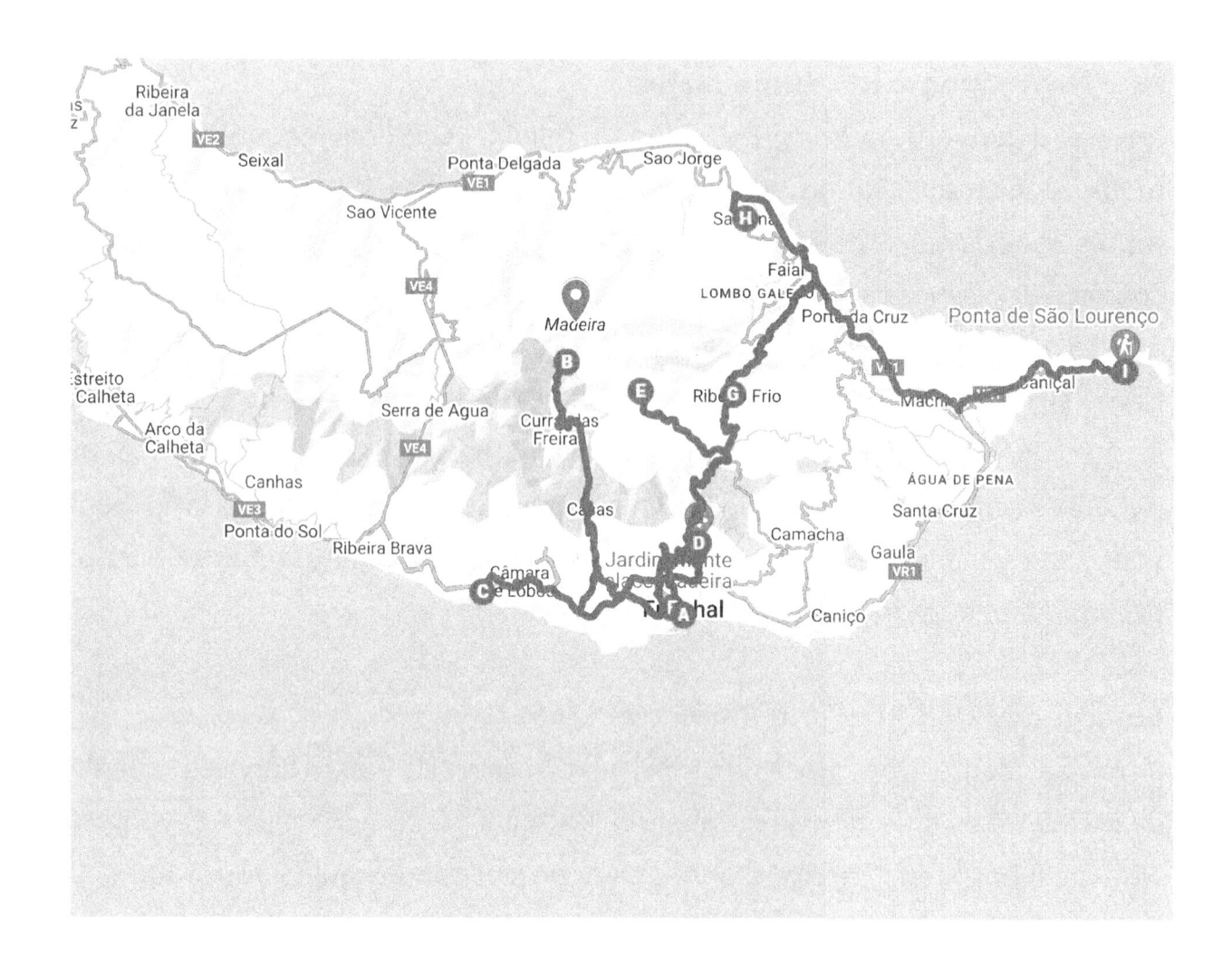

4.1 Must-Visit Landmarks

Funchal Cathedral

Nestled in the heart of Funchal, the Sé Catedral de Nossa Senhora da Assunção stands as a testament to Madeira's enduring history. Built in the late 15th century, this cathedral exudes Gothic and Moorish influences. The intricate woodwork and silverware inside narrate the island's ecclesiastical journey. The entrance is free, offering visitors a glimpse into the island's spiritual past.

Cabo Girão Skywalk

Perched at 580 meters above sea level, Cabo Girão boasts the highest cliff skywalk in Europe. The glass-floored platform provides an awe-inspiring panoramic view of the Atlantic Ocean and Funchal. Originally a viewpoint for brave adventurers, the skywalk offers an adrenaline-pumping experience. Entry costs around €5, a small price for an unforgettable perspective.

Monte Palace Tropical Garden

Nestled in Monte, this botanical haven unveils the delicate beauty of Madeira's flora. The garden's origins trace back to the late 18th century when the British Consul built his residence here. Today, visitors can stroll through themed gardens, enjoying a diverse collection of exotic plants. The entry fee is approximately €12, granting access to a serene escape into nature's artistry.

Pico do Arieiro

For those seeking panoramic vistas, Pico do Arieiro stands as the third-highest peak in Madeira. A road winds its way to the summit, offering breathtaking views of the island's rugged terrain. On clear days, one can catch a glimpse of Porto Santo Island. The entry is free, making it an accessible yet majestic spot for nature enthusiasts.

Quinta das Cruzes

This 17th-century manor turned museum, Quinta das Cruzes, is a window into Madeira's aristocratic past. Situated in Funchal, it houses an impressive collection of art, furniture, and artifacts. The museum's lush gardens transport visitors to a bygone era of elegance. Entry costs approximately €8, allowing a step back in time through the island's historical legacy.

Ribeiro Frio

Nestled in the heart of Madeira's Laurissilva Forest, Ribeiro Frio offers a serene retreat into nature. The name, meaning "Cold River," alludes to the cool waters flowing through the area. The trout hatchery and walking trails make it a favorite among hikers and nature enthusiasts. Entry is free, making it an accessible and tranquil enclave for visitors.

Santana

Venture to the northeast to discover Santana, renowned for its traditional triangular thatched-roof houses. These quaint abodes, known as palheiros, offer insight into Madeira's rural architecture. The Santana Theme Park provides a cultural immersion into the island's history and traditions. Entry to the park is around €10, a modest price for a journey into Madeira's authentic heritage.

Ponte de São Lourenço

Crossing the Ribeiro Fundo stream, Ponte de São Lourenço stands as a testament to Madeira's engineering prowess. The arch bridge, dating back to the 18th century, connects the villages of São Lourenço and São Jorge. The scenic surroundings and historical significance make it a must-visit landmark, and entry is free.

4.2 Natural Wonders

Pico do Arieiro

Located in the central part of the island, Pico do Arieiro stands as the third-highest peak in Madeira, reaching an elevation of 1,818 meters. Its name translates to "Peak of the Shepherd" in English, echoing the pastoral history of the region. The peak offers an unparalleled panorama of jagged peaks, deep valleys, and the vast expanse of the Atlantic Ocean. Visitors often embark on the challenging yet rewarding hike from Pico do Arieiro to Pico Ruivo, the highest peak, to witness the ethereal sunrise casting a golden glow on the rugged terrain.

Laurissilva Forest

Enveloping the higher altitudes of Madeira, the Laurissilva Forest is a living fossil, a remnant of the laurel forest that once covered Southern Europe 15-40 million years ago. Designated as a UNESCO World Heritage site, this ancient forest blankets the mountain slopes, shrouding the landscape in a mystical green cloak. The laurel trees, ferns, and lichens create a unique ecosystem that is home to endemic species such as the Madeiran long-toed wood pigeon and the elusive Madeiran firecrest. Walking through the Laurissilva Forest is akin to stepping back in time, surrounded by primeval beauty and tranquility.

Porto Moniz Natural Pools

On the northwest coast of Madeira lies the mesmerizing Porto Moniz, renowned for its natural volcanic pools. Formed by lava rocks and the relentless pounding of the Atlantic waves, these pools offer a therapeutic retreat amid stunning ocean views. Visitors can immerse themselves in the crystal-clear waters while the waves crash against the rugged cliffs, creating a symphony of natural sounds. The juxtaposition of the azure pools against the dramatic coastline is a testament to the island's geological marvels.

Curral das Freiras - Valley of the Nuns

Nestled in the heart of Madeira, the Curral das Freiras, or Valley of the Nuns, is a hidden gem surrounded by towering peaks. Legend has it that nuns sought refuge in this secluded valley during pirate raids in the 16th century, giving rise to its evocative name. Accessible through winding mountain roads, the valley offers panoramic vistas and a sense of tranquility that feels worlds away from the bustling coastal towns. The terraced fields, olive groves, and charming village nestled within the valley provide a serene escape for those seeking a taste of rural Madeiran life.

São Vicente Caves - Subterranean Wonders
Beneath the surface of Madeira lies a hidden world waiting to be explored – the São Vicente Caves. Carved by volcanic activity millions of years ago, these subterranean chambers showcase the island's geological history. Stalactites and stalagmites create an otherworldly landscape, and guided tours illuminate the scientific marvels of these caves. The underground journey through these natural formations offers a unique perspective on Madeira's geological evolution.

Cabo Girão - A Cliffside Marvel
Cabo Girão stands tall as one of the highest sea cliffs in Europe, offering an awe-inspiring vantage point on the southern coast of Madeira. Rising to a height of 580 meters, the cliff provides a vertigo-inducing panorama of the Atlantic Ocean and the lush coastal landscape below. Adventurous visitors can experience the thrill of walking on the suspended glass platform, providing an unobstructed view straight down to the sea. The sheer grandeur of Cabo Girão makes it a must-visit for those seeking both natural beauty and a touch of adrenaline.

Monte Palace Tropical Garden
Perched high above Funchal, the capital of Madeira, the Monte Palace Tropical Garden is a testament to the island's botanical diversity. Originally

the grounds of a wealthy British merchant, the garden showcases an extensive collection of exotic plants, including cycads, orchids, and azaleas. The meticulously landscaped terraces offer a harmonious blend of architectural elegance and natural beauty, with viewpoints that frame the city below and the vast expanse of the Atlantic Ocean.

4.3 Museums and Galleries

Funchal's Museum of Natural History
Located in Funchal, the capital of Madeira, the Museum of Natural History provides a captivating journey through the island's unique flora and fauna. Entry costs typically range from €5 to €8. Exhibits showcase endemic species, geological formations, and the island's environmental evolution.

Madeira Contemporary Art Museum
For art enthusiasts, the Madeira Contemporary Art Museum in Funchal is a must-visit. This modern space exhibits a diverse collection of contemporary artworks by local and international artists. Entrance fees range from €4 to €6, making it an accessible cultural experience.

Calheta Sugar Cane Museum
Delve into Madeira's agricultural history at the Calheta Sugar Cane Museum. Situated in a former sugar cane mill, this museum details the island's sugar production legacy. Visitors can explore the machinery and learn about the impact of sugar on Madeira's economy. Entry costs typically range from €3 to €5.

Funchal's Sacred Art Museum
Religious and art enthusiasts alike will appreciate the Sacred Art Museum in Funchal. Housed in a former bishop's palace, the museum displays an

extensive collection of religious artifacts, including sculptures, paintings, and liturgical objects. Entry fees are usually around €4 to €7.

Madeira Ethnographic Museum

To understand the island's cultural roots, the Madeira Ethnographic Museum in Ribeira Brava provides a comprehensive exploration. Exhibits cover traditional crafts, folklore, and everyday life, offering insight into Madeira's past. Entry costs range from €3 to €6.

Porto Santo Christopher Columbus House Museum

Venturing to Porto Santo, a neighboring island, visitors can explore the Christopher Columbus House Museum. The museum is housed in the purported birthplace of the famed explorer and offers a glimpse into his life and voyages. Entry fees are generally around €4 to €8.

Madeira Photography Museum

Photography enthusiasts will find a haven in the Madeira Photography Museum in Funchal. Showcasing the evolution of photography on the island, the museum features historical cameras and a diverse array of captivating images. Entry costs typically range from €3 to €5.

4.4 Hidden Gems

São Vicente Caves

Descend into the heart of Madeira's geology with a visit to the São Vicente Caves. Located on the northern coast, these subterranean wonders unravel the island's volcanic past. The intricate labyrinth of caves unveils captivating stalactite formations, with hues ranging from pristine whites to rich amber. The underground river that meanders through the caverns adds an auditory dimension to the experience, creating a symphony of nature's own composition.

Rabaçal Levada Walks

Venture into the mystical Rabaçal Valley for an enchanting hike along the Levada trails. The network of levadas, centuries-old irrigation channels, crisscross the landscape, offering an immersive journey through emerald-green landscapes. The 25 Fontes and Risco Waterfall trails stand out, leading to a natural amphitheater where a cascade of waterfalls descends from the sheer cliffs. This hidden gem provides a serene escape into Madeira's untouched wilderness.

Pico do Arieiro

For a panoramic perspective of Madeira's rugged beauty, ascend to Pico do Arieiro. The third-highest peak on the island, it boasts unparalleled vistas of craggy peaks, lush valleys, and the expansive Atlantic beyond. As the sun paints the sky in hues of orange and pink during sunset, the summit becomes a sanctuary of serenity, offering a profound connection with Madeira's awe-inspiring natural grandeur.

Calhau das Achadas

Escape the tourist hustle to discover the secluded Calhau das Achadas. Nestled on the northwestern coast, this hidden cove enchants with its tranquil pebble beach and crystal-clear waters. The backdrop of towering cliffs and the absence of crowds create an intimate setting, inviting visitors to savor the serenity of Madeira's untouched maritime beauty.

Santana

Embark on a journey to the village of Santana, where traditional triangular thatched houses known as 'casas de colmo' transport visitors to a bygone era. Surrounded by emerald hills, this charming hamlet epitomizes Madeira's rural simplicity. Stroll through cobbled streets adorned with vibrant flowers, and immerse yourself in the authentic local culture that defines this hidden gem.

Fanal

Fanal, a mystical laurel forest in the heart of Madeira, enchants with its ancient trees and ethereal atmosphere. Moss-covered branches create a fairy-tale setting, especially when mist descends, transforming the landscape into a realm of enchantment. As sunlight filters through the dense canopy, Fanal becomes a haven for those seeking tranquility amidst nature's timeless elegance.

4.5 Local Festivals and Events

Madeira Carnival

The festivities kick off with the Madeira Carnival, a colorful extravaganza that takes place in the capital city, Funchal, usually in February or March. The streets come alive with parades, vibrant costumes, and rhythmic music, creating an electrifying atmosphere. The main highlight is the grand parade on Avenida do Mar, where locals showcase elaborate floats and dance to the infectious beat of traditional Madeiran music.

Madeira Flower Festival

As spring blooms across the island, the Madeira Flower Festival graces Funchal in April. This event transforms the city into a floral wonderland, with streets adorned with intricate flower carpets. The main attraction is the Flower Parade, featuring floats decorated with a myriad of colorful blooms.

Visitors can witness the crowning of the Flower Festival Queen, adding a touch of royalty to this botanical celebration.

Atlantic Festival

In June, the Atlantic Festival takes center stage, marking the beginning of summer. The festival spans the entire month, with various events taking place along Funchal's waterfront. The highlight is the International Fireworks Competition, where pyrotechnic displays light up the night sky, captivating audiences with a symphony of colors. The festival also includes live music performances, street food stalls, and a diverse range of cultural activities.

Madeira Wine Festival

As summer unfolds, the Madeira Wine Festival graces the island in August, paying homage to the region's renowned fortified wine. Funchal becomes a hub of wine-related activities, including grape treading, traditional folk music, and wine tastings. The event culminates in the historical Wine Parade, where locals dressed in traditional attire carry baskets of grapes through the streets, celebrating the island's winemaking heritage.

Columbus Festival

September brings the Columbus Festival, commemorating Christopher Columbus' visit to Porto Santo, a neighboring island of Madeira, in 1478. The festival unfolds in Vila Baleira, the capital of Porto Santo, featuring historical reenactments, traditional music and dance, and a maritime procession. Visitors can immerse themselves in the island's seafaring history through exhibitions and cultural events that bring the past to life.

Madeira Nature Festival

For nature enthusiasts, the Madeira Nature Festival in October offers a unique blend of adventure and exploration. The event encourages eco-friendly activities such as hiking, canyoning, and bird watching, allowing participants to discover the island's diverse landscapes. Various excursions and workshops showcase Madeira's commitment to environmental conservation, making it an ideal festival for those seeking a deeper connection with the island's natural beauty.

Madeira Film Festival

Film enthusiasts flock to Madeira in December for the Madeira Film Festival, held in Funchal. This cinematic celebration showcases a selection of international and local films, providing a platform for emerging filmmakers. The festival's unique venues, including open-air screenings against the backdrop of the Atlantic Ocean, create a memorable experience for attendees passionate about the art of cinema.

Christmas and New Year's Eve Celebrations

As the year comes to a close, Madeira transforms into a winter wonderland during the festive season. Funchal is adorned with Christmas lights, and the streets come alive with carolers and seasonal decorations. The highlight is the world-famous New Year's Eve fireworks display, recognized by the Guinness World Records as the largest in the world. Locals and visitors gather along the waterfront to witness the sky illuminated with a breathtaking symphony of fireworks, welcoming the new year in unparalleled style.

CHAPTER 5

PRACTICAL INFORMATION AND TRAVEL RESOURCES

5.1 Maps and Navigation

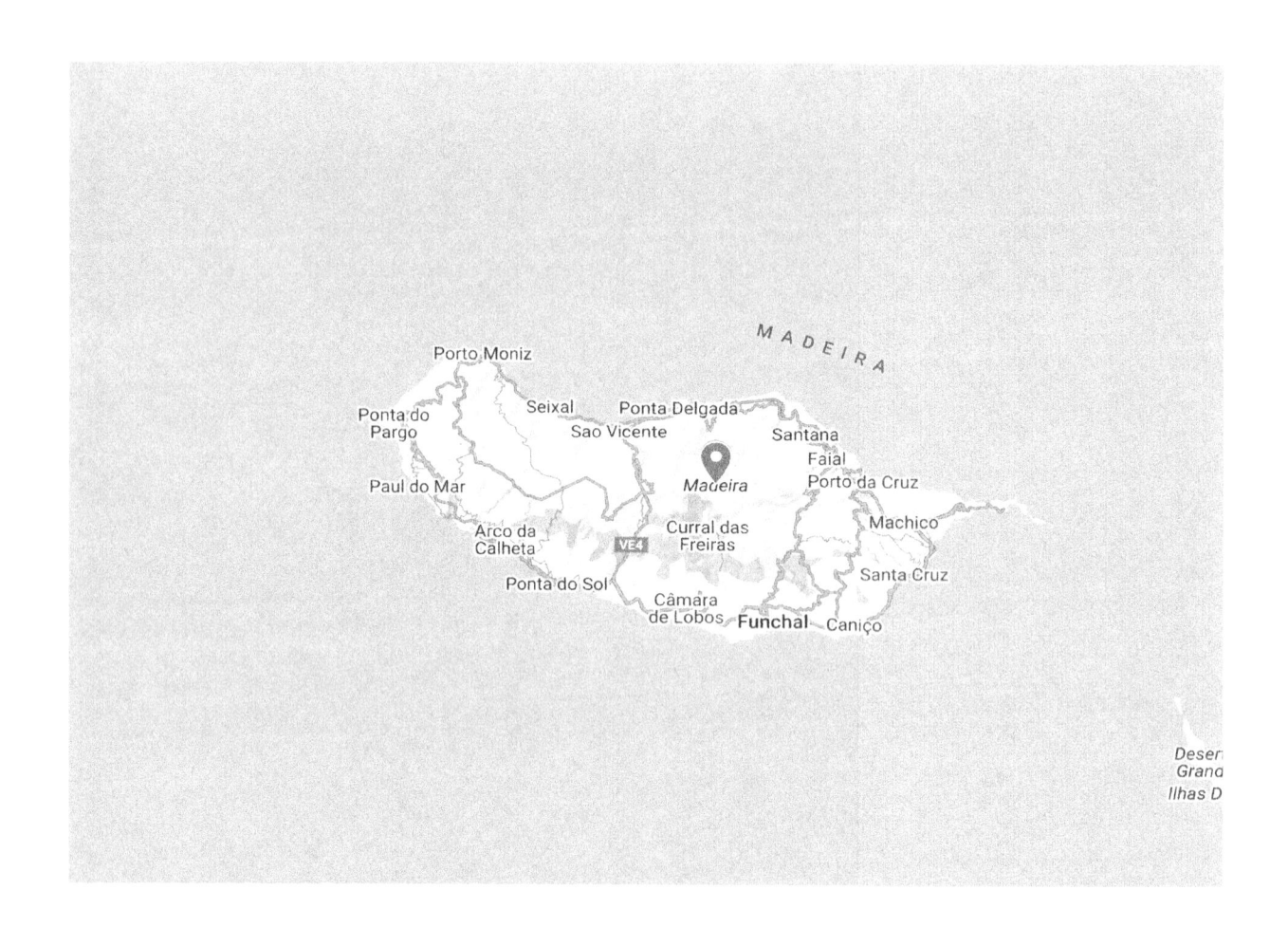

The Geographical Tapestry

Madeira's topography is a masterpiece crafted by nature, and understanding its nuances is paramount for an immersive experience. The island is characterized by steep cliffs, dense forests, and quaint villages, creating a mosaic of diverse terrains. Maps serve as a gateway to unlocking these treasures, offering a visual narrative of the island's geographical tapestry.

Cartographic Gems

Madeira boasts a plethora of cartographic gems that guide the wandering soul. Start your journey with the official maps provided by local tourism authorities, offering a comprehensive overview of the island's regions, roads, and points of interest. Delve deeper into specialized hiking maps for those eager to traverse the island's renowned levadas – irrigation channels turned scenic walking paths. These detailed maps unveil hidden trails and showcase the mesmerizing flora and fauna along the way.

Digital Navigation Tools

In the digital age, navigating Madeira has been revolutionized by technology. Smartphone applications such as GPS navigation apps and travel guides offer real-time assistance. These tools not only provide turn-by-turn directions but also highlight notable landmarks, restaurants, and viewpoints, ensuring a seamless and enriching exploration. However, it's wise to supplement digital aids with traditional maps to navigate areas with limited connectivity.

Navigating Levadas

Levadas, a network of irrigation channels, are synonymous with Madeira's landscape. Navigating these intricate waterways requires a delicate balance of preparedness and appreciation for nature's wonders. Specialized levada maps are essential companions for those seeking to traverse these enchanting paths. These maps reveal the varying difficulty levels of each route, ensuring hikers choose an adventure aligned with their capabilities.

Orientation Amidst Funchal's Charms

Funchal, the vibrant capital of Madeira, presents its own set of navigational delights. The city's cobbled streets wind through historic neighborhoods, adorned with colorful houses and charming markets. While exploring on foot is a delightful option, obtaining a detailed map of Funchal aids in discovering its hidden gems – from the iconic Mercado dos Lavradores to the picturesque Jardim Municipal.

Navigational Etiquette

As visitors embark on their Madeiran odyssey, it's imperative to embrace responsible navigation. Stay attuned to local regulations, especially in ecologically sensitive areas. Levadas, for instance, require a heightened sense of responsibility – stick to designated paths, respect the flora and fauna, and leave no trace. This harmonious approach ensures that future generations can relish the island's natural splendor.

Beyond Maps

While maps guide one through physical landscapes, cultural navigation is equally vital in Madeira. Engaging with locals and immersing oneself in the island's traditions enhances the travel experience. Seek out festivals, taste local delicacies, and explore historical sites to truly understand Madeira's soul. This cultural navigation complements traditional map usage, providing a holistic understanding of the island.

5.2 Essential Packing List

Apparel for All Occasions

Madeira's diverse topography, ranging from the rugged mountains to the sun-kissed beaches, demands a versatile wardrobe. Begin with breathable, moisture-wicking clothing for comfortable exploration of the Levadas, the intricate irrigation channels that crisscross the island. Sturdy hiking boots are essential for traversing the challenging terrains, while swimwear is a must for enjoying the azure waters of the Atlantic. Pack a mix of layers to adapt to varying temperatures, as the island experiences microclimates. A lightweight waterproof jacket is handy for unexpected rain showers, and a sun hat and sunglasses provide protection during sunny days. Don't forget a comfortable pair of walking shoes for strolling through the charming streets of Funchal, the capital city.

Tech Essentials

While Madeira offers a respite from the hustle and bustle, staying connected and capturing the mesmerizing landscapes is still essential. Ensure your smartphone is equipped with a reliable international SIM card to navigate and share your experiences effortlessly. A portable charger or power bank is invaluable for keeping your devices charged during day-long explorations. Consider bringing a compact camera with a good zoom lens to capture the breathtaking scenery, from the panoramic views atop Pico do Arieiro to the vibrant botanical gardens. Don't forget the necessary adapters for charging your devices, as Madeira typically uses European-style power outlets.

Health and Safety Essentials

Prioritize your well-being by packing a small first aid kit that includes essentials like adhesive bandages, pain relievers, and any necessary prescription medications. The island's remote areas might not have immediate access to medical facilities, so it's wise to be prepared for minor health concerns. Include a compact travel insurance document in your essentials, covering potential medical emergencies and unexpected travel disruptions. Familiarize yourself with the local emergency numbers and the location of the nearest healthcare facilities.

Travel-Friendly Toiletries

Opt for travel-sized toiletries to save space in your luggage. Sunscreen with a high SPF is crucial for protecting your skin from the intense Madeiran sun.

Insect repellent can also be handy, especially if you plan on exploring the more wooded areas of the island. Pack a compact, quick-drying towel for beach days and a reusable water bottle to stay hydrated while exploring. A toiletry bag with compartments will help keep your essentials organized and easily accessible.

Culinary Explorations

Madeira is renowned for its delectable cuisine, and you'll want to savor the local flavors to the fullest. While dining out is a delightful experience, having a reusable water bottle and a compact, reusable cutlery set can be convenient for on-the-go snacks and picnics. Consider packing a small snack bag with energy bars or nuts for those moments between meals. Don't forget to sample the local specialties like espetada (skewered meat) and indulge in the world-famous Madeira wine.

Navigational Aids

Given the diverse landscapes and the intricate network of trails, having reliable navigational aids is crucial. Include a detailed map of the island and a compass for hiking expeditions. While modern technology provides convenience, having a traditional map can be a reliable backup in areas with limited connectivity. Consider downloading offline maps and navigation apps to your smartphone to assist with real-time directions. A small, durable backpack is perfect for carrying your essentials during day trips, providing ample space for snacks, water, and your navigation tools.

Cultural Etiquette and Language

Immerse yourself in the local culture by respecting Madeira's customs and traditions. Pack a pocket-sized phrasebook or language translation app to help bridge any language barriers. Learning a few basic Portuguese phrases will be appreciated by the locals and enhance your overall experience. Respectful attire is essential, especially when visiting religious sites or participating in local events. Pack a lightweight scarf or shawl for covering shoulders when needed, ensuring you can comfortably engage in cultural activities.

5.3 Safety Tips and Emergency Contacts

Understanding the Terrain

Madeira's diverse terrain, characterized by steep cliffs and winding roads, demands a cautious approach. Whether trekking through the Levadas or navigating the island's roads, a keen awareness of the surroundings is paramount. Adequate footwear, especially for hikers, is crucial to prevent slips and falls.

Weather Precautions

Madeira experiences a mild climate, but sudden weather changes are not uncommon. Travelers should stay informed about the local weather forecast and be prepared for unexpected rain or wind. Carrying a light waterproof jacket and appropriate gear can make a significant difference in ensuring a comfortable and safe experience.

Emergency Contacts

Emergency Services (112): The universal emergency number, 112, connects travelers with immediate assistance. Whether it's a medical emergency, fire, or any life-threatening situation, dialing 112 ensures a swift response from the local emergency services.

Health Line (808 24 24 24): This contact provides medical advice and information. Travelers can seek guidance on health-related concerns, ensuring that they receive timely assistance and are directed to the appropriate healthcare facilities if needed.

Tourist Support Line (800 296 296): Designed specifically for tourists, this hotline offers support in various situations. Whether it's lost documents, travel-related queries, or any general assistance, the Tourist Support Line is a valuable resource for visitors.

Police (291 208 400): In case of any legal or security issues, contacting the local police is essential. This number connects tourists with law enforcement, ensuring a prompt response to incidents and concerns.

Madeira Civil Protection (291 700 112): Specializing in disaster management and civil protection, this contact is crucial in situations like natural disasters or large-scale emergencies. It serves as a central hub for coordinating responses and ensuring the safety of residents and visitors alike.

Navigating Transportation Safely

Whether renting a car or using public transport, following safety guidelines is vital. Stay alert on mountainous roads, adhere to speed limits, and use designated stops for public transport. Additionally, ensure that vehicles are in good condition, and if relying on public transport, be aware of the schedules and routes to avoid any inconvenience.

Cultural Sensitivity and Respect

Respecting local customs and traditions is not only a cultural courtesy but also contributes to personal safety. Understanding and following the local etiquette helps travelers navigate social situations with ease, minimizing the risk of misunderstandings or conflicts.

Water Safety

Madeira's coastline offers mesmerizing views and opportunities for water-related activities. However, currents can be strong, and caution is advised when swimming or participating in water sports. Always adhere to designated swimming areas, wear appropriate safety gear, and be mindful of changing tides.

Hiking Etiquette

Madeira's network of Levadas provides enchanting hiking trails. However, it's essential to stick to marked paths, carry a map, and inform someone about your hiking plans. Weather conditions in mountainous areas can change rapidly, so being prepared with essentials like water, snacks, and appropriate clothing is crucial.

5.4 Currency, Banking, Budgeting and Money Matters

Currency in Madeira

Madeira, like mainland Portugal, utilizes the Euro (€) as its official currency. Travelers can conveniently exchange their currency at various locations across the archipelago, including banks, currency exchange offices, and ATMs. It's advisable to be aware of the current exchange rates to make informed financial decisions during your trip.

Banking Facilities

Madeira provides a reliable and accessible banking infrastructure, ensuring that visitors have convenient options for managing their finances. Major banks on the island include Banco Santander Totta, Caixa Geral de

Depósitos, and Millennium bcp. These institutions offer a range of services, including currency exchange, ATM access, and assistance with financial transactions.

ATMs in Madeira

ATMs are widely available throughout Madeira, especially in urban areas and popular tourist destinations. Travelers can withdraw Euros from ATMs using international credit or debit cards. However, it's essential to notify your bank of your travel dates to avoid any potential issues with card transactions. Additionally, check for any associated fees with international withdrawals.

Banking Hours and Locations

Typically, banks in Madeira operate on weekdays from 8:30 AM to 3:00 PM. Some branches may close during lunch hours, so it's advisable to plan visits accordingly. Visitors can find banks in various locations, with prominent branches in Funchal, the capital city. Exact addresses can be obtained from the respective bank's website or local information centers.

Currency Exchange Offices

Apart from banks, visitors can utilize currency exchange offices for converting their money. These offices are often found in tourist-centric areas, major hotels, and near popular attractions. While exchange rates may vary slightly, these establishments offer convenient alternatives to banking facilities.

Budgeting Tips for Travelers

Effectively managing your budget is crucial for a fulfilling experience in Madeira. Consider the following tips:

Daily Expenses: Plan your daily expenses for accommodation, meals, transportation, and activities. While Madeira offers a range of options, setting a daily budget helps control spending.

Dining Options: Explore local markets and eateries to experience authentic Madeiran cuisine at affordable prices. This allows you to savor the island's flavors without breaking the bank.

Transportation: Consider purchasing a transportation pass or opting for public transport to explore the island economically. Rental cars are also available for those who prefer flexibility in their travel itinerary.

Entrance Fees: Research attractions beforehand to determine entrance fees and plan accordingly. Some locations may offer discounts for advance bookings or combination tickets.

Souvenirs: Allocate a specific budget for souvenirs and local products. This ensures that you bring home memorable items without overspending.

5.5 Language, Communication and Useful Phrases

Portuguese as the Dominant Language
Portuguese serves as the official language of Madeira, reflecting the island's historical ties with Portugal. While English is widely understood in tourist areas, embracing a few Portuguese phrases can foster a deeper connection with the local culture.

Greetings and Polite Expressions
Upon arriving in Madeira, it's customary to exchange warm greetings. "Bom dia" (Good morning), "Boa tarde" (Good afternoon), and "Boa noite" (Good

evening/night) are commonly used expressions that showcase politeness. When interacting with locals, using "por favor" (please) and "obrigado/a" (thank you) adds a gracious touch to conversations.

Navigating Everyday Situations

For travelers, it's valuable to be equipped with phrases that facilitate everyday interactions. Inquiring about directions may involve asking, "Onde fica?" (Where is?) or "Como chego a...?" (How do I get to...?). When exploring local markets or shops, the phrase "Quanto custa?" (How much does it cost?) becomes handy. Engaging in basic conversations about preferences can involve expressions like "Gosto de..." (I like) or "Não gosto de..." (I don't like).

Dining Etiquette and Culinary Phrases

Madeira boasts a rich culinary scene, and engaging in dining etiquette can enhance the gastronomic experience. When entering a restaurant, a polite greeting like "Boa noite, uma mesa para dois, por favor" (Good evening, a table for two, please) sets a positive tone. Expressing dietary preferences can be done with phrases like "Sou vegetariano/a" (I am a vegetarian) or "Sem glúten" (Gluten-free).

Cultural Events and Expressions

Attending cultural events in Madeira is a delightful way to immerse oneself in the local atmosphere. During festivals or performances, common expressions include "Que espetáculo maravilhoso!" (What a wonderful show!) or "Estou a adorar" (I'm loving it). Demonstrating appreciation for local art and music fosters a connection with the island's vibrant cultural scene.

Emergency Situations and Safety Phrases

While exploring Madeira's natural beauty, being prepared for unforeseen circumstances is crucial. Knowing phrases such as "Ajuda!" (Help!), "Chame uma ambulância" (Call an ambulance), or "Onde está a farmácia mais próxima?" (Where is the nearest pharmacy?) can be invaluable in emergency situations, ensuring prompt assistance.

Public Transportation and Travel Phrases

Navigating public transportation is made easier with essential travel phrases. Asking about bus schedules can be done with "Qual é o horário do autocarro?" (What is the bus schedule?), while purchasing tickets may involve saying "Um bilhete para Funchal, por favor" (One ticket to Funchal, please). Expressing gratitude to the driver with "Obrigado/a pelo trajeto seguro" (Thank you for the safe journey) is a courteous practice.

Socializing and Making New Connections

Madeira's welcoming atmosphere encourages social interactions. Initiating conversations with locals can be enhanced by saying "Posso juntar-me a vocês?" (May I join you?) or "Estou a adorar a vossa companhia" (I'm enjoying your company). Learning a few friendly expressions like "É um prazer conhecer-te" (It's a pleasure to meet you) fosters positive connections.

Exploring Nature and Outdoor Phrases

Madeira's natural beauty beckons exploration, and understanding outdoor phrases enhances the experience. Asking about hiking trails can involve saying "Qual é a trilha mais bonita?" (What is the most beautiful trail?), while expressing awe at scenic views can be done with "Que vista incrível!" (What an incredible view!).

Participating in Local Traditions

Engaging in local traditions deepens the cultural experience. During festivals or celebrations, expressing good wishes with "Feliz Natal" (Merry Christmas) or "Feliz Ano Novo" (Happy New Year) aligns with Madeiran traditions. Participating in traditional dances or rituals opens doors to a richer understanding of the island's heritage.

5.6 Useful Websites, Mobile Apps and Online Resources

Travel Planning

Visit Madeira (https://www.visitmadeira.pt/): The official tourism website offers a wealth of information on attractions, accommodations, and events. Explore the interactive map, plan your itinerary, and discover hidden gems.

Lonely Planet Madeira(https://www.lonelyplanet.com/portugal/madeira): For insightful travel guides, tips, and reviews, Lonely Planet remains a go-to resource. Their Madeira section provides detailed information on everything from local cuisine to hiking trails.

Accommodations

Booking.com (https://www.booking.com/): Whether you prefer a cozy guesthouse or a luxury resort, Booking.com provides a vast array of accommodation options with user reviews to help you make informed decisions.

Airbnb (https://www.airbnb.com/): For a more personalized experience, consider Airbnb. From charming cottages to city apartments, you can find unique stays that suit your preferences.

Transportation

Madeira Airport (https://www.aeroportomadeira.pt/): Stay updated on flight schedules, airport services, and essential travel information through the official Madeira Airport website.

Moovit App (https://moovitapp.com/): Navigating Madeira's public transportation is made easier with Moovit. Access real-time bus schedules, routes, and even plan your journey in advance.

Outdoor Activities

Trailforks App (https://www.trailforks.com/): If you're an avid hiker or mountain biker, Trailforks provides detailed trail maps and user reviews to help you explore Madeira's stunning landscapes.

Madeira Levada Walks (https://www.walkmeguide.com/): Discover the famous levada walks with this online guide. Detailed descriptions, difficulty levels, and trail maps ensure a seamless hiking experience.

Dining and Cuisine

Zomato (https://www.zomato.com/): Uncover the best dining spots in Madeira through Zomato. Read reviews, explore menus, and find restaurants that cater to your culinary preferences.

Madeira Wine (https://www.visitmadeira.pt/en-gb/what-to-do/madeira-wine): Immerse yourself in Madeira's rich wine culture with this online resource.

Learn about local vineyards, wine tasting events, and the history of Madeira wine.

Language and Communication

Google Translate App (https://translate.google.com/): Overcome language barriers with the Google Translate app. Download the Portuguese language pack for offline use and easily communicate with locals.

Duolingo (https://www.duolingo.com/): Brush up on your Portuguese language skills before your trip with Duolingo's interactive language learning platform.

5.7 Visitor Centers and Tourist Assistance

Funchal Visitor Center

The bustling capital city, Funchal, hosts the primary gateway for tourists. The Funchal Visitor Center, situated near the waterfront, serves as a hub for essential information. Knowledgeable staff provides details on local attractions, transportation options, and accommodation recommendations. Additionally, the center offers maps, brochures, and personalized assistance to help visitors tailor their Madeira experience.

Airport Tourist Assistance

For those arriving by air, the Airport Tourist Assistance desk ensures a smooth transition from the moment travelers land. Located within the arrivals area, this facility offers information on airport services, transportation, and immediate recommendations for exploring Madeira. It acts as a welcoming introduction, making visitors feel at ease as they embark on their island adventure.

Regional Tourist Information Offices

Beyond Funchal, various regional tourist information offices dot the archipelago, providing localized insights. Notable locations include Machico, Santana, and Porto Santo. These offices offer region-specific details, highlighting unique attractions, cultural events, and culinary delights. Visitors can access tailored advice based on their chosen destinations within Madeira.

Nature Reserves and Parks Centers

Madeira's natural beauty is one of its most alluring features. Nature reserves and parks, such as Laurissilva Forest and Pico do Arieiro, host dedicated information centers. These locations cater to nature enthusiasts, offering details on hiking trails, flora, and fauna. Knowledgeable guides are often available to enhance the outdoor experience.

Interactive Online Platforms

In the digital age, tourists can supplement their on-site assistance with interactive online platforms. Madeira Tourism's official website and mobile applications provide real-time updates, interactive maps, and virtual guides. These resources empower visitors to plan their itineraries, discover hidden gems, and stay informed about local events.

Multilingual Support

Recognizing the diverse influx of visitors, Madeira's tourist assistance services prioritize multilingual support. English, Spanish, and German are commonly spoken at these centers, ensuring effective communication and understanding between staff and tourists. This commitment to linguistic diversity enhances the overall visitor experience.

Cruise Ship Information Centers

Given Madeira's popularity as a cruise ship destination, specialized information centers cater to maritime travelers. Located near the ports, these centers offer tailored advice for cruise passengers, including shore excursions, local cuisine recommendations, and transportation options for exploring the islands during their stopovers.

CHAPTER 6

CULINARY DELIGHTS

6.1 Traditional Madeiran Cuisine

Madeira is not only renowned for its stunning landscapes and vibrant culture but also for its distinctive and delectable traditional cuisine. The island's gastronomy is a reflection of its history, geography, and the blending of various cultural influences over centuries. As visitors embark on a culinary journey through Madeira, they are treated to a captivating array of flavors, textures, and aromas that define the essence of this picturesque island's food culture.

Bolo do Caco: The Quintessential Madeiran Bread

A staple in Madeiran cuisine, Bolo do Caco is a type of flat, circular bread that has become synonymous with the island's culinary identity. Prepared using sweet potatoes, flour, water, and a touch of salt, this bread is traditionally cooked on a caco, a flat basalt stone, which imparts a unique flavor and texture. Bolo do Caco is often enjoyed with garlic butter, local cheeses, or as an accompaniment to various traditional dishes. Visitors can find this iconic bread at local bakeries, markets, and even in street stalls across the island.

Espetada: Skewering the Island's Flavors

Espetada, a savory delight that has its roots in Madeira's rich agricultural heritage, is a dish that exemplifies the island's love for grilled meats. Typically made with marinated beef or fish, the skewered delicacy is seasoned with garlic, bay leaves, and a dash of local spices. Grilled to perfection over an open flame, espetada is often served with the island's staple side dish, milho frito (fried maize), and a refreshing salad. Visitors can relish this traditional dish in local restaurants and taverns, where the aroma of grilling meats fills the air, creating an authentic Madeiran dining experience.

Lapas com Cebola: Savoring the Ocean's Bounty

Madeira's connection to the Atlantic Ocean is vividly reflected in its seafood offerings, and Lapas com Cebola is a prime example of the island's culinary celebration of oceanic treasures. Lapas, or limpets, are small marine mollusks abundantly found along Madeira's rocky shores. Cooked with onions, garlic, and a blend of aromatic herbs, lapas com cebola captures the essence of the sea. This dish is a favorite among locals and can be savored in seaside eateries, where the rhythmic crashing of waves provides a serene backdrop to a seafood feast.

Bife de Atum: Tuna Steaks Madeiran Style

Tuna is a culinary gem in Madeira, and Bife de Atum, or tuna steak, showcases the island's mastery in preparing this versatile fish. Sourced locally from the Atlantic waters surrounding Madeira, tuna steaks are seasoned with Madeiran spices and grilled to perfection. Often accompanied by batata doce frita (sweet potato fries) and a medley of fresh vegetables, Bife de Atum is a nutritious and flavorful dish that exemplifies the island's commitment to sustainable and locally-sourced ingredients.

Traditional Madeiran Desserts: A Sweet Culmination

No exploration of Madeiran cuisine is complete without indulging in the island's delightful desserts. Queijada, a sweet pastry made with fresh cheese, eggs, sugar, and a hint of cinnamon, is a popular treat among locals and visitors alike. Additionally, passion fruit mousse, known as maracujá, tantalizes the taste buds with its tropical richness. These desserts can be found in local bakeries and dessert shops, adding a sweet note to the culinary journey through Madeira.

Traditional Madeiran Cuisine is a testament to the island's rich history, geographical bounty, and a deep connection to its cultural roots. From the iconic Bolo do Caco to the tantalizing Bife de Atum, each dish tells a story of tradition, innovation, and a love for locally-sourced ingredients. As visitors savor the flavors of Madeira, they not only nourish their bodies but also embark on a sensory journey that encapsulates the essence of this enchanting island in the Atlantic.

6.2 Popular Dishes and Snacks

As travelers set foot on the enchanting island of Madeira, they are not only greeted by the breathtaking landscapes but also by a cornucopia of delectable dishes and snacks that define the local culinary scene. A fusion of traditional flavors, innovative techniques, and the bountiful offerings of the Atlantic Ocean, Madeira's popular dishes and snacks provide a gastronomic journey that is as diverse as the island itself.

Bolo do Caco: A Taste of Madeiran Heritage

No exploration of Madeiran cuisine is complete without savoring the iconic Bolo do Caco. This traditional bread, prepared with sweet potatoes, flour, water, and a touch of salt, is a staple that has stood the test of time. Baked on a flat basalt stone, known as a caco, it acquires a distinct flavor and texture. Bolo do Caco is commonly found in local bakeries, markets, and street stalls, often served with garlic butter or accompanying the island's famed espetada.

Espetada: Skewering Madeiran Flavors

Espetada, a culinary masterpiece born from Madeira's agricultural heritage, is a dish that captures the essence of grilled meats. Typically featuring marinated beef or fish skewered and grilled to perfection, espetada is seasoned with garlic, bay leaves, and local spices. This savory delight is often paired with milho frito (fried maize) and a refreshing salad. Visitors can indulge in the mouthwatering flavors of espetada at local restaurants and taverns, where the aroma of grilling meats permeates the air.

Lapas com Cebola: Oceanic Treasures on the Plate

Lapas com Cebola is a testament to Madeira's strong connection to the Atlantic Ocean. These small marine mollusks, known as limpets, are cooked with onions, garlic, and aromatic herbs, creating a dish that celebrates the island's abundant seafood. Savored in seaside eateries, the dish offers a sensory experience where the crashing waves provide a harmonious backdrop to the flavors of the ocean.

Bife de Atum: Tuna Steaks, Madeiran Style

Tuna, a prized catch from the surrounding Atlantic waters, takes center stage in Madeira's culinary repertoire with Bife de Atum. Tuna steaks, seasoned with local spices, are grilled to perfection and often served with sweet potato fries and fresh vegetables. This dish not only tantalizes the taste buds but also embodies Madeira's commitment to sustainable and locally-sourced ingredients.

Queijada and Maracujá: A Sweet Culmination

For those with a sweet tooth, Madeira offers delightful desserts that showcase the island's passion for confectionery. Queijada, a sweet pastry made with fresh cheese, eggs, sugar, and a hint of cinnamon, is a popular treat found in local bakeries. Additionally, maracujá, or passion fruit mousse, adds a tropical and refreshing note to the dessert scene. These sweet indulgences can be enjoyed in various eateries and dessert shops across the island.

As visitors traverse the culinary landscape of Madeira, they will discover a harmonious blend of tradition, innovation, and a commitment to fresh, locally-sourced ingredients. From the heritage-rich Bolo do Caco to the ocean-inspired Lapas com Cebola and the succulent Bife de Atum, each dish tells a unique story, inviting visitors to embark on a sensory journey that captures the heart and soul of this picturesque island in the Atlantic.

6.3 Dining Etiquette

Madeira, the enchanting archipelago in the Atlantic Ocean, not only captivates visitors with its stunning landscapes and vibrant culture but also beckons them into a world of exquisite gastronomy. Dining in Madeira is not merely a sustenance ritual; it is a celebration of heritage, a symphony of flavors that resonates with the island's rich history. As a visitor, immersing oneself in the local dining etiquette becomes an integral part of the Madeiran experience.

I. Traditional Culinary Delights: A Gastronomic Prelude

Before delving into the nuances of dining etiquette, it is essential to familiarize oneself with the gastronomic treasures that await. Madeira boasts a fusion of Portuguese, African, and Moorish influences, resulting in a unique and delectable cuisine. From the renowned "espetada" skewers of marinated meats to the iconic "bolo do caco" bread, the island's culinary repertoire reflects a harmonious blend of tradition and innovation.

II. The Laid-back Charm of Madeiran Dining Atmosphere

Madeiran dining establishments, whether humble family-run taverns or upscale restaurants, share a common trait – a laid-back charm that invites patrons to savor their meals at a leisurely pace. Unlike the hurried pace of some urban centers, dining in Madeira encourages guests to relish the moment, engage in unhurried conversations, and fully appreciate the flavors that grace their palates.

III. Respecting Meal Times: A Synchrony with Tradition

In Madeira, meal times adhere to a rhythmic cadence that aligns with the island's cultural traditions. Lunch, typically the main meal of the day, is enjoyed between 1:00 PM and 3:00 PM, while dinner is a more relaxed affair, starting around 8:00 PM. Visitors are encouraged to embrace this cultural norm, allowing them to partake in the island's culinary offerings in harmony with its temporal rhythms.

IV. Embracing Local Customs: An Etiquette Overture

Respecting local customs is paramount in Madeira, and this extends to the dining table. A customary greeting before meals involves a friendly "Bom apetite!" (Good appetite!), demonstrating not only politeness but a shared appreciation for the forthcoming culinary delights. Moreover, it is customary to leave a small amount of food on one's plate as a sign of satisfaction, rather than an indication of dissatisfaction, which might be misconstrued in other cultures.

V. Wine Culture: Navigating the Vineyard of Choices

Madeira is renowned for its wines, and no dining experience is complete without indulging in the island's vinous offerings. The local "Madeira wine" is a fortified wine that comes in various styles, from dry to sweet. When selecting a wine, seeking guidance from the knowledgeable waitstaff is not only acceptable but encouraged. Additionally, it is customary to offer a toast before commencing the meal, expressing gratitude and camaraderie.

VI. Dress Code Elegance: Adorning Attire with Respect

Dining in Madeira often transcends mere sustenance; it is an opportunity to showcase a sense of elegance and respect for the culinary experience. While the island embraces a casual atmosphere, especially in beachside eateries, it is advisable for visitors to don smart-casual attire when venturing into upscale restaurants, ensuring they seamlessly blend with the refined ambiance.

VII. Tipping Practices: Expressing Gratitude with Generosity

Tipping is a customary practice in Madeiran dining establishments. While a service charge is often included in the bill, leaving an additional 5-10% as a token of appreciation for exceptional service is a gesture that resonates well with the local culture. This expression of gratitude further cements the connection between visitor and host, emphasizing the shared enjoyment of the culinary journey.

VIII. The Culmination: Desserts and Coffee Rituals

No Madeiran dining experience is complete without indulging in the island's delectable desserts and engaging in the post-meal ritual of coffee. The "queijada" and "bolo de mel" are popular choices for those with a sweet tooth, while a cup of robust locally-roasted coffee serves as the perfect denouement to the culinary symphony.

In conclusion, dining etiquette in Madeira is not a rigid set of rules but a dance of traditions, flavors, and respect. By immersing oneself in the island's culinary customs, visitors embark on a gastronomic journey that goes beyond the mere satisfaction of hunger – it becomes a celebration of culture, tradition, and the shared joy of a well-enjoyed meal.

6.4 Recommended Restaurants

The island of Madeira not only enchants visitors with its natural beauty but also tantalizes their taste buds with a diverse array of culinary delights. Exploring the recommended restaurants on this picturesque island provides a gateway to a gastronomic adventure, where local flavors, innovative techniques, and warm hospitality converge to create an unforgettable dining experience.

Canto das Fontes: A Riverside Culinary Retreat

For those seeking a dining experience that seamlessly blends Madeiran flavors with an idyllic setting, Canto das Fontes stands as a beacon of culinary excellence. Situated along the riverbank in Ribeira Brava, this restaurant offers panoramic views of the water and surrounding mountains. Renowned for its seafood specialties, Canto das Fontes curates a menu that showcases the freshest catches from the Atlantic, complemented by locally-sourced ingredients. The ambiance, coupled with attentive service, elevates the overall dining experience, making it a must-visit for those desiring a perfect blend of nature and gastronomy.

Il Gallo d'Oro: Michelin-Starred Elegance

In the heart of Funchal, Il Gallo d'Oro stands proudly as one of Madeira's Michelin-starred gems. Located within The Cliff Bay Hotel, this restaurant, under the guidance of Chef Benoît Sinthon, offers a gastronomic journey that transcends traditional boundaries. The menu, characterized by a fusion of Madeiran, Iberian, and Mediterranean influences, presents a symphony of flavors that delight the palate. The elegant ambiance and meticulous attention to detail make Il Gallo d'Oro a destination for those seeking a Michelin-starred culinary experience in Madeira.

Armazém do Sal: A Historic Culinary Haven

In the heart of Funchal's historic Old Town, Armazém do Sal beckons diners with its rich history and culinary prowess. Housed in a former salt warehouse, the restaurant seamlessly combines the charm of its heritage with a contemporary dining experience. Armazém do Sal is celebrated for its commitment to showcasing Madeiran ingredients, with dishes that pay homage to the island's culinary traditions. The outdoor terrace, surrounded by cobblestone streets and historic buildings, adds a touch of romanticism to the dining atmosphere, making it an ideal spot for an evening of gastronomic indulgence.

O Regional: Embracing Authentic Madeiran Cuisine

For an authentic Madeiran culinary journey, O Regional in the heart of Funchal stands as a testament to preserving local flavors. This charming restaurant, adorned with traditional décor, offers a menu that reflects the island's gastronomic heritage. From the iconic Espetada to the beloved Bolo do Caco, O Regional's culinary repertoire captures the essence of Madeira's culinary identity. The warm and welcoming atmosphere, coupled with friendly service, makes O Regional a go-to destination for those craving a genuine taste of Madeira.

Gaviao Novo: A Fusion of International and Madeiran Flavors

Perched on the cliffs of Ponta do Sol, Gaviao Novo presents a unique fusion of international and Madeiran flavors against the backdrop of the Atlantic. With a diverse menu that caters to various palates, this restaurant is a favorite among locals and visitors alike. The panoramic views of the ocean, coupled with a carefully curated wine list, create an atmosphere of refined relaxation. Gaviao Novo is an ideal choice for those seeking a culinary journey that embraces both global influences and the distinct tastes of Madeira.

Exploring the recommended restaurants in Madeira is not merely a gastronomic adventure but a cultural immersion into the heart and soul of the island. Each establishment, with its unique setting, diverse menu, and commitment to local ingredients, contributes to the tapestry of Madeiran cuisine. From riverside retreats to Michelin-starred elegance, these culinary oases invite visitors to savor the flavors of Madeira in an atmosphere of warmth, sophistication, and genuine hospitality.

6.5 Food Festivals and Markets

At the heart of Madeira's capital, Funchal Food Market stands as a testament to the island's bustling culinary scene. This market, also known as Mercado dos Lavradores, is a vibrant kaleidoscope of colors, aromas, and flavors. Opened in the 1930s, the market is a treasure trove of fresh produce, local delicacies, and traditional crafts. Visitors can meander through stalls brimming with exotic fruits, aromatic spices, and freshly caught seafood, providing a sensory journey into the island's gastronomic diversity.

Festival do Atlântico: A Culinary Extravaganza

Each summer, Madeira transforms into a stage for the Festival do Atlântico, a month-long celebration that transcends beyond its name to embrace various cultural elements, including a culinary extravaganza. The festival features a series of events, from open-air concerts to spectacular fireworks displays, but it is the gastronomic offerings that steal the spotlight. Restaurants and stalls across the island showcase their culinary prowess, offering a diverse range of dishes that highlight Madeira's traditional flavors and innovative twists.

Madeira Wine Festival: A Toast to Tradition

For wine enthusiasts, the Madeira Wine Festival is an annual highlight that pays homage to the island's renowned fortified wine. Held in Funchal, this event typically takes place in late August and early September. The festival includes a ceremonial parade, where locals adorned in traditional costumes carry barrels of wine through the city streets. Visitors can partake in wine tastings, explore vineyards, and learn about the meticulous process behind the production of Madeira wine. The festival culminates in a vibrant street party, creating an atmosphere of revelry and camaraderie.

Banana Festival: Honoring a Tropical Treasure

The Banana Festival, held in Madalena do Mar, is a testament to the importance of bananas in Madeira's agricultural landscape. This charming event typically takes place in September, showcasing the island's banana cultivation through exhibitions, tastings, and lively parades. Visitors can learn about the different banana varieties grown on the island, indulge in banana-themed dishes, and immerse themselves in the vibrant festivities that underscore the significance of this tropical fruit in Madeiran culture.

Chestnut Festival: Embracing Autumn's Bounty

As autumn colors paint the landscapes of Madeira, the Chestnut Festival takes center stage, celebrating the abundance of chestnuts that flourish on the island. Typically held in Curral das Freiras, this event invites locals and visitors alike to revel in the seasonal splendor. The festival features chestnut roasting, traditional music and dance performances, and a culinary showcase where chestnuts are incorporated into a variety of dishes, from savory stews to sweet desserts.

In conclusion, exploring the food festivals and markets in Madeira is an immersive journey into the heart of the island's culinary identity. From the bustling stalls of Funchal Food Market to the cultural extravagance of the Festival do Atlântico, each event offers a unique lens through which visitors can savor the flavors, traditions, and community spirit that define Madeiran cuisine. As the island comes together to celebrate its gastronomic heritage, travelers are not only treated to exquisite fare but are invited to become a part of the vibrant tapestry of Madeira's culinary legacy.

CHAPTER 7

CULTURE AND HERITAGE

7.1 Arts and Crafts

Madeira, a Portuguese archipelago known for its breathtaking landscapes and vibrant culture, has cultivated a distinctive arts and crafts scene that captivates visitors from around the world. This essay delves into the diverse artistic traditions and crafts that flourish on this picturesque island, providing a comprehensive guide for those eager to immerse themselves in the local creative spirit.

Traditional Embroidery: A Stitch in Time

One of the most iconic and cherished art forms in Madeira is traditional embroidery. Renowned for its intricate designs and meticulous craftsmanship, Madeiran embroidery has deep roots in the island's history. Visitors can explore the charming ateliers and boutiques where skilled artisans passionately bring to life intricate patterns, inspired by the island's flora and fauna. The vibrant colors and delicate stitches tell stories of tradition and heritage, making each piece a unique work of art. For those seeking a tangible connection to Madeira's cultural legacy, acquiring a piece of locally crafted embroidery is a must.

Wickerwork: Weaving Nature's Bounty

Venturing into the heart of Madeira's arts and crafts scene, wickerwork emerges as a captivating expression of the island's connection to nature. Skilled craftsmen transform locally sourced materials, such as willow and cane, into functional and aesthetically pleasing pieces. Visitors can witness the intricate process of weaving, where baskets, furniture, and decorative items come to life. The unique blend of tradition and innovation in Madeiran wickerwork reflects the island's commitment to preserving its cultural identity while embracing contemporary design.

Ceramics: Molding Timeless Beauty

The art of ceramics has a profound presence in Madeira, seamlessly blending utilitarian and artistic elements. Local artisans mold clay into exquisite pottery, reflecting the island's maritime heritage and natural beauty. From intricately designed plates to decorative tiles, each piece tells a story of craftsmanship passed down through generations. Visitors can explore the workshops and studios, witnessing the delicate dance between tradition and modernity in the creation of these timeless ceramic treasures.

Lace Making: Threads of Heritage

Madeira's lace-making tradition is another jewel in its artistic crown. Delicate and intricate, Madeiran lace reflects the island's historical ties to Europe. Skilled artisans, often found in charming villages, continue to create exquisite lacework using time-honored techniques. Visitors have the opportunity to observe the meticulous process and gain insight into the cultural significance of this delicate craft. Acquiring a piece of Madeiran lace serves not only as a beautiful memento but also as a testament to the island's commitment to preserving its rich heritage.

Art Galleries and Studios: A Contemporary Expression

While deeply rooted in tradition, Madeira's arts and crafts scene is not confined to the past. The island boasts a vibrant contemporary art scene with numerous galleries and studios showcasing the work of local and international artists. From avant-garde exhibitions to traditional paintings inspired by the island's landscapes, these spaces offer a diverse range of artistic expressions. Exploring these venues provides visitors with a nuanced understanding of Madeira's evolving artistic identity and its integration with global creative currents.

Culinary Arts: A Feast for the Senses

In Madeira, the arts extend beyond the visual and tactile to embrace the culinary realm. Local markets brim with fresh produce, offering a sensory journey into the island's gastronomic delights. Culinary artisans craft traditional dishes like espetada (skewered meat) and bolo do caco (sweet potato bread), inviting visitors to savor the flavors of Madeira's unique cultural tapestry. Engaging in culinary experiences, such as cooking classes or food tours, provides a holistic appreciation of Madeira's artistic expressions.

Exploring the arts and crafts of Madeira unveils a rich tapestry woven from the threads of tradition, innovation, and creativity. The island beckons visitors with the promise of a cultural journey, inviting them to witness the hands that shape timeless crafts and the minds that weave contemporary narratives. Whether immersing oneself in the delicate art of embroidery, the sturdy beauty of wickerwork, the timeless allure of ceramics, or the intricate elegance of lace, Madeira's artistic landscape is an invitation to connect with a living, breathing cultural heritage. The island's commitment to preserving its artistic legacy while embracing modern influences ensures that every visitor leaves with not just a souvenir, but a lasting impression of a place where art transcends time.

7.2 Historical Sites

Madeira beckons visitors with not only its natural beauty but also a rich tapestry of historical sites that bear witness to centuries of captivating history. Immerse yourself in the allure of the past as we explore the island's remarkable historical landmarks, each narrating tales of exploration, conquest, and cultural exchange.

Funchal's Historic Heart: Sé Cathedral and Santa Clara Convent

Begin your historical odyssey in Funchal, the capital city, where the Sé Cathedral stands as a testament to the island's religious heritage. A masterpiece of Gothic architecture, the cathedral dates back to the 15th century, adorned with intricate carvings and beautiful azulejos. Adjacent to the cathedral, the Santa Clara Convent, founded in the early 16th century, unveils the austere beauty of Franciscan architecture and offers a tranquil retreat within the bustling city.

Fortresses and Coastal Defenses: A Glimpse into Madeira's Strategic Past

Explore Madeira's strategic significance at the historic fortresses and coastal defenses scattered across the island. The São Tiago Fortress in Funchal, constructed in the 17th century, served as a formidable defense against pirate attacks. Perched on the coastline, Forte do Pico and Forte de São João Baptista in Funchal and Ponta do Sol, respectively, provide panoramic views of the Atlantic and insights into the island's maritime history. These fortifications evoke the era when Madeira was a crucial outpost in the Atlantic, guarding against naval threats.

Mercado dos Lavradores: A Vibrant Hub of Commerce Through the Ages

Step into the Mercado dos Lavradores, Funchal's bustling market, where history mingles with the vibrancy of daily life. Dating back to the 1930s, this market is a living testament to Madeira's agricultural heritage. Stroll through its colorful aisles, marveling at fresh produce, exotic flowers, and regional crafts. The lively atmosphere and architectural charm make it not just a market but a living chapter in the island's social and economic history.

Quinta das Cruzes: A Glimpse into Madeira's Noble Past

For a taste of Madeira's aristocratic history, venture to Quinta das Cruzes, a splendid mansion turned museum in Funchal. This 17th-century estate, once owned by João Gonçalves Zarco, one of the island's original discoverers, showcases a rich collection of art, furniture, and artifacts. Wander through meticulously maintained gardens, absorbing the ambiance of a bygone era and gaining insight into the lifestyle of Madeira's elite.

Pico do Arieiro: Scaling the Heights of History and Nature

Ascend to Pico do Arieiro, the third-highest peak in Madeira, for an immersive experience that combines history and breathtaking natural vistas. Here, remnants of the island's pre-Portuguese history come alive through the ancient footpaths and rock formations. Traversing the rugged terrain, visitors encounter cairns and markers left by early settlers, offering a glimpse into the island's mystical past.

São Vicente Caves and Volcanism Center: Unveiling Earth's Geological Story

Delve into the geological history of Madeira at the São Vicente Caves and Volcanism Center. These subterranean caverns, formed by volcanic activity, provide a fascinating insight into the island's volcanic origins. The Volcanism Center complements the cave experience with interactive exhibits, educating visitors about the geological forces that shaped Madeira's dramatic landscapes over millions of years.

Madeira's historical sites weave a captivating narrative that spans centuries, from the island's discovery to its role in maritime defense and agricultural prosperity. Whether exploring Gothic cathedrals, fortresses overlooking the

Atlantic, or delving into the geological mysteries beneath the surface, each site invites visitors to step back in time. Immerse yourself in the historical tapestry of Madeira, where the echoes of the past resonate through architectural wonders, cultural landmarks, and natural formations, leaving indelible imprints on the traveler's soul.

7.3 Local Art Scene

Madeira is not only a haven for nature enthusiasts but also a thriving hub of artistic expression. The local art scene, rich in diversity and inspiration, invites visitors to delve into a world where creativity knows no bounds. Let's embark on a journey through the kaleidoscope of Madeira's vibrant artistic community, where traditional craftsmanship meets contemporary innovation.

Traditional Crafts and Artisanal Mastery: Ateliers and Workshops

One of the defining features of Madeira's art scene lies in its traditional crafts, passed down through generations with unwavering dedication. Artisanal ateliers and workshops dot the island, offering visitors the chance to witness the meticulous process behind crafts like embroidery, wickerwork, and ceramics. Engaging with skilled artisans provides not just a visual spectacle but an immersive experience, fostering a deeper appreciation for the artistry embedded in Madeira's cultural heritage.

Contemporary Art Galleries: Where Innovation Meets Tradition

Funchal, the vibrant capital of Madeira, is home to a burgeoning contemporary art scene. Galleries such as the Art Center Caravel and Arc Gallery showcase the works of local and international artists, pushing the boundaries of creativity. Visitors can explore exhibitions ranging from traditional paintings inspired by Madeira's landscapes to avant-garde installations that challenge perceptions. These spaces act as dynamic canvases, reflecting the evolving narrative of Madeira's artists within the global context of contemporary art.

Street Art: A Canvas Unfolding in Public Spaces

The streets of Funchal and other towns on the island serve as open-air galleries, where vibrant murals and street art pieces infuse urban spaces with color and meaning. Talented local artists, inspired by Madeira's landscapes and culture, transform blank walls into dynamic expressions of creativity. Strolling through these streets becomes a journey of discovery, uncovering hidden gems that seamlessly blend tradition with modernity, turning the entire island into a canvas waiting to be explored.

Cultural Festivals: Celebrating Art in All its Forms

Madeira's art scene comes alive during cultural festivals that celebrate various forms of creative expression. The Madeira Film Festival, for instance, brings filmmakers from around the world to showcase their work against the stunning backdrop of the island. Similarly, the Madeira Literary Festival invites authors and literature enthusiasts to engage in discussions and workshops. These events not only provide a platform for artists but also offer visitors the opportunity to participate in the lively cultural tapestry of Madeira.

Artisan Markets: A Showcase of Local Talent and Craftsmanship

For those seeking to bring a piece of Madeira's artistry home, artisan markets provide a treasure trove of unique creations. From handmade jewelry to locally designed clothing, these markets offer a direct connection to the island's creative pulse. Mercado da Arte in Funchal, for instance, showcases a diverse array of locally crafted items, allowing visitors to support local artists while acquiring one-of-a-kind souvenirs.

Artistic Retreats: Nurturing Creativity Amidst Nature's Bounty

Madeira's inspiring landscapes have attracted artists seeking solitude and inspiration for centuries. The island offers artistic retreats where painters, writers, and creators can immerse themselves in the natural beauty of the surroundings. These retreats provide an opportunity for visitors to engage with artists, attend workshops, and witness the fusion of nature and creativity in real-time.

Madeira's local art scene weaves a captivating tapestry that combines the richness of tradition with the dynamism of contemporary expression. Visitors can traverse the island, discovering the hands that craft intricate traditional pieces, exploring galleries that push artistic boundaries, and engaging with the vibrant street art that decorates urban landscapes. The local art scene in Madeira beckons, inviting travelers to become a part of a creative journey where inspiration knows no limits.

7.4 Traditional Music and Dance

Immersing oneself in the cultural heartbeat of Madeira goes beyond scenic landscapes and historical landmarks; it extends to the enchanting world of traditional music and dance. The island's rich musical heritage, shaped by its history and vibrant community spirit, provides visitors with a unique opportunity to engage in an auditory and rhythmic journey that is both captivating and deeply rooted in tradition.

Fado Madeirense: The Soulful Lament of Madeira's Heart

At the core of Madeira's traditional music is "Fado Madeirense," a soul-stirring genre that speaks to the island's emotional landscape. Originating from Portuguese roots, Fado Madeirense weaves tales of love, saudade (longing), and the profound connection to the sea. The haunting melodies, accompanied by the plaintive chords of the Portuguese guitar and the expressive tones of the singer, create an intimate and emotional experience for listeners. Visitors have the opportunity to witness live performances in local taverns and cafes, where Fado singers pour their hearts into each note, inviting audiences to connect with the raw emotions embedded in this musical tradition.

Bailinho da Madeira: A Dance of Joy and Heritage

Complementing the soulful melodies of Fado Madeirense is the lively tradition of "Bailinho da Madeira," a colorful and exuberant folk dance that reflects the island's joyous spirit. Dancers clad in traditional costumes adorned with vibrant embroidery move in rhythmic patterns, echoing the lively tunes of accordion, drums, and other traditional instruments. The dance, often performed during festivals and celebrations, invites visitors to join in the jubilant atmosphere, experiencing firsthand the communal energy that defines Madeira's cultural gatherings.

Traditional Instruments: Echoes of the Past in Musical Notes

Madeira's traditional music is brought to life by an array of unique instruments that carry the echoes of the island's past. The Brinquinho, a small accordion-like instrument, and the Rajão, a small guitar, are integral to the melodic tapestry of Fado Madeirense. The rhythmic beats of the Brinquinho, coupled with the melodic strumming of the Rajão, create a distinctive sound that resonates with the island's cultural identity. Visitors keen on exploring the roots of Madeira's musical heritage can engage with local musicians and instrument makers, gaining insight into the craftsmanship behind these traditional instruments.

Festivals and Celebrations: A Musical Extravaganza

For an immersive experience of Madeira's musical traditions, attending local festivals and celebrations is a must. The Festa da Flor, celebrating the blooming of spring, and the lively Carnival are occasions where traditional music and dance take center stage. The streets come alive with the sounds of Fado Madeirense and the rhythmic steps of Bailinho da Madeira, creating an infectious atmosphere of celebration and cultural pride. Visitors can join the festivities, partaking in the joyous dance and reveling in the harmonies that echo through the cobbled streets.

Cultural Centers and Performances: Preserving and Showcasing Heritage

Madeira's commitment to preserving its musical heritage is evident in cultural centers and dedicated performances that showcase traditional music and dance. The Municipal Theatre Baltazar Dias in Funchal often hosts events featuring local musicians and dance troupes, providing a platform for artists to share their talents with both locals and visitors. These performances offer a curated experience, allowing audiences to appreciate the nuances of Madeira's musical traditions in a more formal setting.

The traditional music and dance of Madeira offer visitors a harmonious invitation to explore the island's cultural depths. From the soulful strains of Fado Madeirense to the lively rhythms of Bailinho da Madeira, the auditory landscape of the island is as diverse as its picturesque scenery. Engaging with traditional music and dance becomes a gateway to understanding the heart and soul of Madeira's people, fostering a connection that transcends time. For those seeking a truly immersive cultural experience, Madeira's musical traditions stand ready to enchant and captivate, promising an unforgettable journey through the rhythmic melodies of tradition.

7.5 Celebrating Madeiran Culture

Madeira, an island paradise in the Atlantic, beckons visitors not only with its natural beauty but also with a rich tapestry of cultural traditions that have stood the test of time. As you step onto this enchanting terrain, be prepared to immerse yourself in a celebration of Madeiran culture that spans music, dance, festivals, and culinary delights, promising an unforgettable experience.

Fado Nights: Soulful Echoes of Madeiran Emotion

To truly understand the heartbeat of Madeira, one must delve into the soul-stirring melodies of Fado Madeirense. Nights come alive with the haunting tunes of this traditional music, echoing through the cobbled streets of Funchal. Taverns and cafes offer intimate settings for live performances, where Fado singers pour their hearts into each note, sharing stories of love, longing, and the profound connection to the sea. Attendees are not mere spectators but active participants in an emotional journey, connecting with the raw sentiments embedded in the fabric of Madeiran culture.

Bailinho da Madeira: A Dance of Joy and Unity

The lively tradition of "Bailinho da Madeira" encapsulates the island's joyous spirit and communal energy. Vibrant folk dance performances, adorned with traditional costumes and accompanied by accordion and drums, invite both locals and visitors to join in the rhythmic celebration. Attending a traditional dance event, whether during a local festival or at a cultural center, offers an opportunity to witness the vivacity of Madeiran culture firsthand. The spirited movements and contagious joy create an atmosphere where cultural unity is not just observed but experienced.

Festivals: A Kaleidoscope of Colors and Traditions

Madeira's festivals are vibrant celebrations that showcase the island's cultural diversity. The Festa da Flor, celebrating the blooming of spring, transforms the streets into a riot of colors with floral displays and parades. The Carnival, marked by elaborate costumes and lively processions, captivates both young and old. These festivals are not just spectacles; they are immersive experiences that allow visitors to engage with Madeiran traditions, taste local delicacies, and dance to the rhythmic beats that reverberate through the festive air.

Craftsmanship: The Artistry of Madeiran Hands

A significant aspect of Madeiran culture lies in its traditional craftsmanship, where skilled artisans bring age-old techniques to life. Whether exploring ateliers for intricate embroidery, workshops for wickerwork, or studios for ceramics, visitors have the chance to witness the meticulous process behind each craft. Acquiring a handmade piece not only serves as a tangible memento but also as a connection to the hands that have preserved Madeira's cultural identity through centuries.

Culinary Delights: A Feast for the Senses

No exploration of Madeiran culture is complete without indulging in its culinary delights. From the robust flavors of Espetada (skewered meat) to the sweet allure of Bolo do Caco (sweet potato bread), the island's gastronomy reflects its diverse influences. Local markets, such as the Mercado dos Lavradores, offer a sensory journey into Madeira's food culture. Engaging in cooking classes or partaking in food tours allows visitors to not only savor the flavors but also understand the stories behind each dish, making the culinary experience an integral part of celebrating Madeiran culture.

Local Markets: A Cultural Marketplace

For those seeking authentic experiences, Madeira's local markets are cultural marketplaces where tradition and commerce intertwine. Mercado dos Lavradores in Funchal is a prime example, where fresh produce, regional crafts, and the vibrant atmosphere converge. Navigating through these markets is not just a shopping spree; it's an opportunity to interact with locals, understand the significance of local products, and witness the dynamic exchanges that define Madeiran daily life.

In conclusion, celebrating Madeiran culture is not a mere observation; it's an immersive odyssey into the heart and soul of the island. Whether through the emotional resonance of Fado, the lively dances of Bailinho da Madeira, the kaleidoscope of festivals, the craftsmanship of local artisans, or the culinary feasts that tantalize the taste buds, every aspect beckons visitors to become active participants in the cultural tapestry. Madeira, with its warmth, diversity, and enduring traditions, invites you to not just witness but to be a part of its cultural celebration, ensuring that every visitor departs with memories of a truly enriching cultural experience.

CHAPTER 8

OUTDOOR ACTIVITIES AND ADVENTURES

8.1 Hiking and Trekking Trails

Madeira, with its dramatic landscapes and lush terrain, is a haven for hiking enthusiasts seeking to explore nature at its finest. The island's extensive network of hiking and trekking trails offers a captivating journey through dense forests, mountain peaks, and coastal cliffs. As you lace up your hiking boots, get ready to discover the diverse trails that wind through this breathtaking Atlantic gem.

Levada Walks: Tracing Waterways Amidst Verdant Landscapes

No exploration of Madeira's hiking trails is complete without delving into the intricate network of levadas. These are ancient irrigation channels that crisscross the island, providing a unique foundation for hiking paths. Levada walks offer a tranquil journey through lush laurel forests, picturesque valleys, and hidden waterfalls. The Levada do Caldeirão Verde, with its emerald green surroundings, and the Levada do Risco, leading to the iconic 100-meter high Risco waterfall, are must-visit trails for those craving an immersive experience with nature.

Pico Ruivo: Scaling the Island's Highest Peak

For the adventurous soul, the trek to Pico Ruivo is a pinnacle experience. As the highest peak on Madeira, Pico Ruivo rewards hikers with panoramic views that stretch across the island and the surrounding ocean. The trail, often shrouded in mist, adds an ethereal touch to the journey. The challenging yet rewarding ascent is a testament to Madeira's diverse landscapes, transitioning from rocky paths to alpine meadows, providing an unparalleled sense of accomplishment.

Vereda do Areeiro: A High-Altitude Adventure

Connecting the peaks of Areeiro and Ruivo, the Vereda do Areeiro trail offers a high-altitude adventure for those seeking an adrenaline rush. The path winds through mountainous landscapes, offering breathtaking vistas and a sense of serenity. As you traverse this trail, the ever-changing weather and the rugged beauty of the surroundings create an awe-inspiring experience that captures the essence of Madeira's untamed natural splendor.

Rabaçal: Enchanting Waterfalls and Laurissilva Forests

The Rabaçal valley is a treasure trove for hikers, boasting enchanting waterfalls and the ancient Laurissilva forest. Trails like the Rabaçal to 25 Fontes and Risco provide a magical journey through lush greenery, leading to cascading waterfalls and crystal-clear lagoons. The sound of water trickling through the Laurissilva trees adds a soothing melody to the hike, creating an immersive experience that transports hikers into a world of natural wonder.

São Lourenço Peninsula: Coastal Beauty Unveiled

For a different perspective, the São Lourenço Peninsula trail introduces hikers to the rugged beauty of Madeira's coastline. With the Atlantic on one side and dramatic cliffs on the other, this trail offers a contrasting landscape that combines the azure sea with arid terrain. The diversity of flora and fauna, along with the refreshing sea breeze, adds a unique flavor to the hiking experience, making it a must for those seeking coastal adventures.

Practical Tips for Hikers: Embracing the Trail with Confidence

Before embarking on these trails, it's essential for visitors to be well-prepared. Sturdy hiking boots, weather-appropriate clothing, and sufficient water are crucial companions. Many trails in Madeira involve varied terrains and altitudes, so having a map or GPS device is advisable. Additionally, checking weather conditions before setting out ensures a safe and enjoyable hiking experience.

Madeira's hiking and trekking trails beckon adventurers with a promise of unparalleled natural beauty and diverse landscapes. Whether wandering through the timeless levadas, conquering the heights of Pico Ruivo, exploring the enchanting Rabaçal valley, or tracing the coastal allure of São Lourenço Peninsula, each trail offers a unique adventure. Madeira, with its well-maintained paths and awe-inspiring vistas, stands as a testament to nature's artistry, inviting hikers to embark on a majestic odyssey through its captivating landscapes. The island's trails promise not only physical exertion but also a spiritual connection with the untamed beauty of this Atlantic gem, ensuring that every hiker departs with memories etched in the soul.

8.2 Water Sports

Strategically positioned in the azure embrace of the Atlantic Ocean, Madeira is not only a sanctuary for nature lovers but also a haven for water sports enthusiasts seeking aquatic adventures. From the thrill of surfing along the rugged coastlines to the serene exploration of underwater wonders, Madeira's diverse water sports scene invites visitors to plunge into an aquatic playground like no other.

Surfing and Bodyboarding: Conquering Atlantic Waves

Madeira's coastline, characterized by dramatic cliffs and pristine beaches, offers an ideal canvas for surfing and bodyboarding aficionados. Jardim do Mar and Paul do Mar, with their consistent swells, are popular spots for surfers of all skill levels. The island's unique geography ensures a variety of wave conditions, catering to both beginners seeking lessons and experienced surfers yearning for a challenging ride. The harmony between the surfer and the Atlantic waves creates an exhilarating experience that captures the essence of Madeira's aquatic allure.

Stand-Up Paddleboarding (SUP): Navigating Coastal Serenity

For a more serene water adventure, stand-up paddleboarding (SUP) in Madeira is an enchanting experience. The calm waters of the island's marinas, such as Funchal's harbor, offer an ideal environment for paddleboarders to glide effortlessly over crystal-clear waters. As you navigate along the coastline, the juxtaposition of cliffs and sea creates a mesmerizing backdrop, making SUP an activity that combines tranquility with the scenic grandeur of Madeira.

Snorkeling and Scuba Diving: Exploring Underwater Marvels

Beneath the surface, Madeira unveils a mesmerizing underwater world teeming with marine life and vibrant coral formations. Snorkeling in spots like Ponta de São Lourenço allows visitors to observe the diverse aquatic ecosystem, including colorful fish and intriguing rock formations. For those seeking deeper exploration, scuba diving excursions are available, offering the chance to discover underwater caves, wrecks, and the rich biodiversity of the Atlantic Ocean.

Kayaking: Coastal Exploration at Your Pace

Kayaking along Madeira's coastlines provides an intimate connection with the island's natural beauty. Paddling through hidden coves and sea arches, kayakers can explore areas inaccessible by land. The island's rugged cliffs and calm bays offer a diverse range of kayaking experiences, from leisurely coastal exploration to more challenging routes for the adventurous at heart. Kayaking allows visitors to appreciate the sheer majesty of Madeira's seascapes, fostering a deep appreciation for the island's coastal wonders.

Whale and Dolphin Watching: Ocean Safaris

Madeira's waters are not only a playground for water sports enthusiasts but also a habitat for diverse marine life. Visitors can embark on ocean safaris for the chance to encounter whales and dolphins in their natural environment. The warm Atlantic currents around Madeira attract various species, including sperm whales, orcas, and playful dolphins. Guided boat tours, departing from Funchal and other coastal towns, provide a memorable opportunity to witness these majestic creatures and learn about marine conservation efforts in the region.

Before indulging in water sports activities, it's essential for visitors to prioritize safety. While many adventure sports operators in Madeira offer equipment rental and guided excursions, ensuring compliance with safety regulations is crucial. Depending on the chosen activity, participants may need to consider factors such as weather conditions, currents, and their own skill levels. Enlisting the services of certified instructors and guides enhances the overall experience, allowing visitors to focus on the enjoyment of their chosen water sports.

Madeira's water sports scene is a dynamic tapestry that weaves together the thrill of surfing, the tranquility of paddleboarding, the exploration of underwater realms, and the excitement of marine encounters. The island's diverse aquatic offerings cater to a spectrum of preferences, from adrenaline-seeking surfers to those seeking a leisurely connection with the sea. As the Atlantic waves beckon, Madeira stands as an irresistible invitation for water sports enthusiasts to dive into an aquatic wonderland, where each adventure promises not only exhilaration but also a deeper appreciation for the mesmerizing beauty of the island's coastal realm.

8.3 Bird Watching

The archipelago of Madeira isn't just a haven for beachgoers and hikers; it's also a paradise for bird enthusiasts. With its diverse ecosystems, including laurel forests, coastal cliffs, and mountainous terrain, Madeira provides a rich habitat for a variety of bird species. Here, bird watching becomes a captivating pursuit, offering visitors a unique opportunity to connect with the island's avian residents.

Rich Avian Biodiversity: A Feathered Tapestry

Madeira's strategic location, along with its varied landscapes, has endowed the island with an impressive avian biodiversity. From endemic species to migratory birds, the skies and lush greenery of Madeira are teeming with feathered inhabitants. Notable species include the Madeira Laurel Pigeon, Zino's Petrel, and the Plain Swift. Bird watchers are in for a treat as they explore different habitats, each offering a chance to spot a diverse array of winged wonders.

Hotspots for Bird Watching: Nature's Theater Unfolds

Several key locations on the island serve as hotspots for bird watching, each presenting a unique theater of nature. The Laurissilva Forest, a UNESCO World Heritage site, is home to endemic birds like the Madeira Firecrest and the Trocaz Pigeon. The rugged cliffs of Ponta de São Lourenço provide a coastal vantage point for observing seabirds, including Cory's Shearwater and Bulwer's Petrel. The diverse environments of the Rabaçal Valley and the Pico do Arieiro offer additional opportunities to encounter various species in their natural habitats.

Best Seasons for Bird Watching: A Year-Round Affair

Madeira's mild climate makes bird watching a year-round activity, but certain seasons offer unique opportunities. Spring and autumn, in particular, are periods of avian activity, with migratory birds passing through or making Madeira their temporary home. During these seasons, the island's landscapes burst with color, providing a picturesque backdrop for bird watchers to enjoy their hobby amidst blooming flowers and verdant foliage.

Bird Watching Tours: Guided Explorations

For those eager to enhance their bird watching experience, guided tours are readily available on the island. Local experts, well-versed in the habits and habitats of Madeira's birdlife, lead enthusiasts to prime locations and share insights about the various species encountered. These tours not only provide a structured approach to bird watching but also contribute to the conservation efforts by promoting responsible observation practices.

Conservation Efforts: Nurturing Avian Habitats

Madeira's commitment to conservation extends to its avian inhabitants. Various initiatives and projects aim to protect and preserve the unique birdlife on the island. Visitors can learn about ongoing conservation efforts, contributing to the broader understanding of how environmental stewardship plays a crucial role in safeguarding Madeira's delicate ecosystems.

Equipment and Etiquette: Essentials for Bird Watching

To make the most of a bird watching excursion, visitors should come prepared with essential equipment such as binoculars, field guides, and comfortable clothing suitable for the outdoors. Practicing ethical bird watching etiquette, which includes minimizing disturbance to the birds and their habitats, ensures a responsible and sustainable approach to this captivating activity.

Madeira's bird watching experience is a harmonious symphony of feathers and nature, inviting enthusiasts to immerse themselves in the island's avian wonders. From the endemic species that call the laurel forests home to the migratory birds gracing the skies during their seasonal travels, Madeira offers a diverse and captivating bird watching experience. For those who appreciate the beauty of flight and the delicate balance of ecosystems, Madeira beckons as a paradise where every fluttering wing becomes a part of a unique and enriching avian tapestry.

8.4 Golf Courses

Madeira is not only renowned for its lush landscapes and vibrant culture but also for its exceptional golf courses that offer a unique blend of challenging play and breathtaking scenery. For enthusiasts seeking an unforgettable golfing experience, Madeira stands out as an ideal destination. Let's delve into the details of these golf courses, exploring their distinctive features and the allure they hold for visitors.

Palheiro Golf: A Symphony of Nature and Elegance

One of Madeira's most distinguished golf courses, Palheiro Golf, is a testament to the island's natural beauty. Situated on an elevated plateau overlooking the capital city, Funchal, this 18-hole course provides a challenging yet enjoyable experience for golfers of all skill levels. The undulating terrain, adorned with centuries-old trees and vibrant flora, creates a stunning backdrop that captures the essence of Madeira's landscape.

As players navigate through the course, they encounter panoramic views of the Atlantic Ocean and Funchal Bay, adding an extra layer of awe to the golfing experience. The course's design, courtesy of renowned golf architect Cabell B. Robinson, seamlessly integrates with the island's topography, creating a harmonious synergy between sport and nature.

Santo da Serra Golf: Where Tradition Meets Championship Quality

For those seeking a more traditional golfing experience, Santo da Serra Golf offers an exceptional journey through Madeira's rich history. Hosting prestigious events such as the Madeira Islands Open, this course boasts 27 holes set within a stunning natural reserve. The meticulously maintained fairways and greens challenge golfers to showcase their skills while surrounded by the island's diverse flora and fauna.

The club's commitment to preserving the environment is evident in its certification as a "Certified Gold Audubon International Signature Sanctuary." This recognition underscores Santo da Serra's dedication to maintaining the delicate ecological balance while providing an exceptional golfing experience.

Porto Santo Golfe: A Secluded Oasis of Tranquility

For those seeking a golfing escape away from the bustling mainland, Porto Santo Golfe, located on the nearby Porto Santo Island, offers a serene retreat. Accessible by a short ferry ride or a quick flight from Madeira, this 18-hole course provides a tranquil setting with unspoiled beaches and dunes framing the fairways.

Designed by the legendary Seve Ballesteros, Porto Santo Golfe combines the natural beauty of the island with a layout that challenges golfers to showcase their strategic prowess. The calming sound of the Atlantic waves and the gentle sea breeze contribute to an unparalleled golfing experience, making it an essential addition to any golf enthusiast's itinerary.

Madeira's Golfing Culture: Beyond the Greens

Beyond the impeccable golf courses, Madeira offers a unique golfing culture that enhances the overall experience for visitors. The island's mild climate ensures year-round playability, making it an attractive destination regardless of the season. Golfers can also indulge in the local culinary delights, savoring fresh seafood and traditional Madeiran dishes at the golf clubs' restaurants.

Moreover, the island's welcoming atmosphere and friendly locals contribute to a memorable stay. Visitors can explore the charming streets of Funchal, visit historic sites, and immerse themselves in the vibrant cultural events that regularly take place.

Madeira stands out not only as a picturesque tourist destination but also as a golfer's paradise. The island's golf courses seamlessly blend with the natural beauty, offering an immersive experience that goes beyond the sport itself. Whether it's the panoramic views at Palheiro Golf, the championship-quality play at Santo da Serra Golf, or the tranquil retreat at Porto Santo Golfe, each course contributes to the allure of Madeira as a premier golfing destination. Embrace the opportunity to tee off amidst nature's splendor and discover why Madeira is a must-visit for golf enthusiasts seeking a perfect blend of challenge and tranquility.

8.5 Exploring Madeira's Natural Beauty

Madeira, an archipelago belonging to Portugal, beckons travelers with its breathtaking natural beauty. This enchanting destination boasts a diverse array of landscapes, from lush green mountains to rugged coastlines, making it an irresistible haven for nature lovers and adventure seekers alike.

Majestic Mountains and Verdant Valleys

One of the defining features of Madeira is its dramatic mountainous terrain. The island's backbone is dominated by the imposing peaks of the Madeira Mountain Range, where the Pico Ruivo stands as the highest point, offering panoramic views that stretch as far as the eye can see. Hiking enthusiasts will find a network of well-maintained trails that crisscross the mountains, allowing them to explore the island's interior and discover hidden valleys adorned with vibrant flora.

Levadas: The Lifelines of Madeira

A unique and iconic feature of Madeira's landscape is its intricate network of levadas. These historic irrigation channels, originally built to supply water to agricultural areas, now serve as picturesque trails winding through the island's forests. Strolling along these levadas provides an intimate encounter with the island's flora and fauna, offering a refreshing escape from the hustle and bustle of daily life.

Enchanting Laurissilva Forests

Declared a UNESCO World Heritage Site, the Laurissilva Forests cover significant portions of Madeira, contributing to its unparalleled biodiversity. This ancient laurel forest, characterized by its evergreen trees and endemic species, provides a habitat for numerous rare and unique plants and animals. Exploring the winding paths beneath the thick canopy, visitors are transported to a primordial world, where time seems to stand still.

Coastal Wonders and Pristine Beaches

Madeira's natural beauty extends to its captivating coastline, where sheer cliffs plunge dramatically into the Atlantic Ocean. The coastal scenery is a spectacle in itself, with natural rock formations and hidden coves waiting to be discovered. The crystal-clear waters surrounding the island are a haven for marine life, making it an ideal destination for snorkeling and diving enthusiasts. Calheta Beach, with its golden sands, offers a tranquil spot to relax and unwind, surrounded by the stunning beauty of the island.

Floral Extravaganza: Madeira's Gardens and Parks

Renowned as the "Floating Garden of the Atlantic," Madeira lives up to its nickname with an abundance of colorful flora. The island's botanical gardens, such as the Monte Palace Tropical Garden and the Madeira Botanical Garden, showcase an impressive collection of both native and exotic plants. Visitors can immerse themselves in a kaleidoscope of colors and fragrances, creating a sensory experience that is both soothing and invigorating.

Culinary Delights Amidst Natural Splendor

Madeira's natural beauty is not limited to its landscapes; it is also reflected in the island's rich culinary heritage. Visitors can indulge in local delicacies, including fresh seafood, succulent fruits, and renowned Madeira wine. The island's quaint villages and charming eateries offer a delightful blend of traditional flavors, allowing visitors to savor the essence of Madeiran cuisine amidst the backdrop of its stunning natural surroundings.

Madeira's natural beauty is a symphony of landscapes that captivates the senses and beckons travelers to immerse themselves in its enchanting allure. From the towering peaks of the mountains to the tranquil beaches, every corner of the island tells a story of nature's artistry. Whether seeking adventure, tranquility, or a culinary journey, Madeira offers a paradise that promises an unforgettable experience. Embrace the call of this Atlantic gem, and let the island's natural wonders weave a tapestry of memories that will linger long after your journey comes to an end.

8.6 Family and Kids Friendly Activities

Madeira, known for its lush landscapes and captivating culture, is not just a destination for adults seeking adventure. Families with children will find an array of family-friendly activities on this Atlantic gem, ensuring a memorable and enriching experience for all members. From nature explorations to interactive cultural encounters, Madeira beckons families to embark on a journey of discovery and joy.

Nature Adventures: A Playground of Natural Wonders

Madeira's natural beauty extends a warm welcome to families, offering a multitude of activities immersed in the island's stunning landscapes. Levada walks, with their gentle paths alongside irrigation channels, provide an ideal setting for family hikes. Trails like Levada do Caldeirão Verde showcase the island's verdant beauty, allowing kids to explore while surrounded by the soothing sounds of nature.

For those seeking a touch of adrenaline, Jeep safaris through the island's diverse terrain offer a family-friendly way to experience the rugged landscapes of Madeira. From the mountains to the coast, these excursions provide not only thrilling rides but also an educational component as knowledgeable guides share insights into the island's flora, fauna, and geological wonders.

Water Parks and Aquatic Delights: Cooling Off in Style

Madeira's warm climate invites families to cool off in style at the island's water parks. The Aquaparque in Santa Cruz, with its water slides, pools, and play areas, promises a day of aquatic fun for children of all ages. Families can relax by the pools, indulge in water activities, and enjoy a delightful escape from the island's sun-drenched afternoons. For a more natural aquatic experience, families can explore Madeira's inviting beaches. Calheta Beach, with its golden sands and calm waters, is particularly family-friendly. The beach offers a safe environment for kids to build sandcastles, paddle in the shallows, or simply bask in the sunshine.

Interactive Museums: Learning Through Play

Madeira's cultural landscape extends to family-friendly museums that offer interactive and educational experiences. The Madeira Story Centre in Funchal engages visitors of all ages with its multimedia exhibits, taking families on a journey through the island's history, culture, and traditions. With hands-on displays and captivating storytelling, children can absorb knowledge in an entertaining and immersive way.

Similarly, the Monte Palace Tropical Garden combines natural beauty with cultural exploration. Families can wander through lush gardens, marvel at exotic flora, and discover the unique Madeiran heritage through art and artifacts. The museum and cultural center within the garden provide additional insights into the island's history and traditions.

Dolphin and Whale Watching: A Maritime Adventure

For families with a sense of adventure, dolphin and whale watching excursions offer a maritime adventure that appeals to all ages. The Atlantic waters surrounding Madeira are home to various species, including dolphins, sperm whales, and orcas. Guided boat tours, departing from Funchal and other coastal towns, provide families with an opportunity to witness these magnificent creatures in their natural habitat. The excitement of spotting marine life creates lasting memories for children and adults alike.

Local Markets and Cultural Experiences: Tastes and Traditions for All Ages

Madeira's vibrant markets, such as the Mercado dos Lavradores in Funchal, are not just shopping destinations but cultural experiences that families can enjoy together. Kids can marvel at the colorful displays of fresh produce, flowers, and local crafts. Engaging with local vendors provides an opportunity for children to learn about Madeira's culinary traditions and crafts, creating a sensory-rich experience. Cultural festivals and events also offer a window into Madeira's lively traditions. The Festa da Flor, with its flower parades, and the Carnival, with colorful costumes and lively processions, are family-friendly celebrations that showcase the island's joyous spirit.

Practical Considerations: Planning for Family Comfort

When planning a family trip to Madeira, considering practical aspects ensures a seamless and enjoyable experience. Accommodations with family-friendly amenities, such as spacious rooms and recreational facilities, contribute to a comfortable stay. Families should also check the accessibility of chosen activities, ensuring that they cater to various age groups. Madeira's warm and welcoming atmosphere extends to its family-friendly dining options. Exploring local restaurants and trying traditional Madeiran dishes can be a delightful way for families to bond over shared meals.

Madeira is not just an island destination; it's a treasure trove of family memories waiting to be created. From nature adventures to water parks, interactive museums, and cultural experiences, Madeira offers a diverse range of family-friendly activities. The island's warm hospitality, coupled with its breathtaking landscapes, ensures that families can embark on a journey of discovery, laughter, and shared experiences. Madeira beckons families to unite in exploration, promising a vacation that fosters connections and creates lasting memories for generations to come.

8.7 Activities for Solo Travelers

Embarking on a solo journey to Madeira is not just an adventure; it's an immersion into a world of diverse landscapes, vibrant culture, and enriching experiences tailored for those seeking solitude and self-discovery. From the scenic coastal cliffs to the lush mountainous terrains, Madeira offers a plethora of activities that cater to the solo traveler's desire for exploration and personal growth.

Hiking and Levada Walks: A Solitary Sojourn Through Nature's Masterpiece

Madeira's network of levadas, narrow irrigation channels that wind through the island, provides solo travelers with an unparalleled opportunity to connect with nature. Hiking along these levadas reveals breathtaking vistas, from cascading waterfalls to ancient laurel forests. For those seeking a solo adventure, the Levada do Caldeirão Verde or the challenging Pico Ruivo hike promises solitude amidst the island's stunning landscapes.

Botanical Gardens and Funchal's Charm: A Solo Stroll Through Floral Paradise

For a leisurely solo day, Funchal, the capital of Madeira, offers charming streets and botanical gardens. Wander through the Jardim Botânico and revel in the beauty of exotic flora, showcasing the island's rich biodiversity. The historic streets of Funchal are perfect for solitary exploration, with quaint cafes, local markets, and historical sites inviting solo travelers to absorb the city's unique atmosphere.

Solo Sea Adventures: Dolphin and Whale Watching

The Atlantic surrounding Madeira is teeming with marine life, and solo travelers can embark on unforgettable sea adventures. Dolphin and whale watching tours provide an opportunity to witness these majestic creatures in their natural habitat. Solo travelers can join group tours, fostering connections with fellow sea enthusiasts, or opt for a more private experience, immersing themselves in the serenity of the open ocean.

Scenic Drives and Sunset Views: A Solo Road Trip

Madeira's winding roads and scenic viewpoints make it an ideal destination for a solo road trip. Renting a car allows travelers to explore the island at their own pace. The iconic Cabo Girão, one of the world's highest sea cliffs, offers a breathtaking vantage point, especially during sunset. Driving along the coastal roads or through the mountainous interior, solo travelers can relish the freedom of the open road.

Culinary Delights for the Solo Palate: Local Gastronomy

Exploring Madeira's culinary scene is a solo adventure in itself. From traditional Madeiran dishes like Espetada and Bolo do Caco to sampling local wines, solo travelers can indulge their taste buds in the island's gastronomic treasures. Visiting local markets, such as the Mercado dos Lavradores in

Funchal, provides an opportunity to interact with vendors and savor fresh, locally sourced produce.

Connecting with Local Culture: Solo Exploration of Madeira's Heritage

Solo travelers keen on delving into Madeira's rich history and culture can visit historical sites and museums. The Madeira Story Centre in Funchal offers an immersive journey through the island's past, while the São Vicente Caves provide a fascinating exploration of volcanic formations. Engaging with locals at cultural events or festivals offers a glimpse into the warm and welcoming spirit of Madeira.

Solo Safety and Practicalities: Navigating Madeira with Confidence

Solo travelers in Madeira can navigate the island with confidence, thanks to its reputation as a safe and tourist-friendly destination. English is widely spoken, and public transportation is reliable for those without a rental car. The island's hospitality extends to solo travelers, making it easy to seek assistance or recommendations from locals.

In conclusion, Madeira beckons solo travelers with a tapestry of activities that promise both solitude and exploration. From the thrill of a solo hike along a levada to the tranquility of a sunset road trip, Madeira's diverse offerings cater to the solo adventurer's desire for self-discovery and meaningful experiences. Whether wandering through botanical gardens, embarking on sea excursions, or savoring local delicacies, a solo journey to Madeira is an opportunity to forge a personal connection with this enchanting island. Embrace the solitude, immerse yourself in the island's beauty, and let Madeira become a haven for your solo travel escapades.

CHAPTER 9

SHOPPING IN MADEIRA

9.1 Souvenirs and Local Crafts

Madeira, a jewel in the Atlantic, invites visitors not only to immerse themselves in its natural wonders but also to partake in the rich tapestry of its local crafts and souvenirs. The island's markets, boutiques, and artisan workshops beckon, promising an authentic shopping experience that reflects the unique cultural heritage of this Portuguese paradise.

Funchal's Vibrant Markets: Mercado dos Lavradores

The heartbeat of Funchal, the capital of Madeira, is the Mercado dos Lavradores, or Farmers' Market. Here, visitors are greeted by a lively mosaic of colors, sounds, and aromas. The market is a treasure trove of locally produced fruits, vegetables, flowers, and handmade crafts. Artisans skillfully display traditional embroidered linens, wicker baskets, and ceramic treasures. Prices vary, allowing visitors to choose from affordable trinkets to more intricate and valuable pieces. The market is not just a shopping destination; it is a cultural immersion where one can engage with local producers and artisans, adding depth to the shopping experience.

Traditional Embroidery: A Time-Honored Craft

Madeira's intricate embroidery has long been a symbol of the island's craftsmanship. Artisans, often working in small ateliers, meticulously create delicate patterns on linens, garments, and accessories. Visitors can explore the charming shops in Funchal, such as Bordal – Madeira Embroidery Factory, to witness the craft firsthand. Prices for embroidered items vary based on complexity and material, ensuring there's something for every budget. These timeless pieces make for exquisite souvenirs, capturing the essence of Madeira's cultural heritage.

Wicker Baskets: Functional Artistry

Wicker weaving, particularly the crafting of "cestos" or baskets, is another longstanding tradition in Madeira. Skilled artisans transform local materials into functional and visually appealing items. The village of Camacha is renowned for its wickerwork, and visitors can purchase baskets of various sizes and designs. The price range accommodates both the budget-conscious traveler and those seeking larger, more intricate pieces. These handwoven baskets not only serve as practical souvenirs but also as lasting symbols of Madeira's artisanal excellence.

Artisanal Ceramics: A Feast for the Eyes

Madeira's red clay is molded into captivating ceramic pieces that seamlessly blend functionality with artistic expression. Visitors can explore pottery workshops, like the Olaria de São Vicente, where artisans showcase their skills. Plates, tiles, and decorative items with unique patterns and designs are available at varying price points. The versatility of these ceramics makes them ideal souvenirs, offering a touch of Madeira's creativity to adorn homes around the world.

Contemporary Art and Jewelry: Funchal's Boutique Scene

Funchal's streets, particularly Rua de Santa Maria, are adorned with boutique shops showcasing contemporary art and handmade jewelry. Local artists contribute to the vibrant scene, offering visitors an opportunity to acquire one-of-a-kind pieces. Prices may vary based on the artist's reputation and the intricacy of the work. Whether it's a painting that captures the essence of Madeira's landscapes or a piece of jewelry inspired by the ocean, these unique creations provide a modern twist to the island's traditional crafts.

Sustainable Souvenirs: Eco-Friendly Choices

As Madeira embraces sustainable practices, visitors can contribute to environmental conservation by choosing eco-friendly souvenirs. Bamboo products, recycled material crafts, and other sustainable items are increasingly available in boutiques and markets. While prices may be slightly higher, these purchases align with the island's commitment to preserving its natural beauty, allowing visitors to take home souvenirs that reflect both the craft and conscience of Madeira.

Shopping for souvenirs and local crafts in Madeira is not merely a transaction but a journey into the soul of the island's vibrant culture and history. Whether exploring Funchal's bustling markets, witnessing the creation of traditional handicrafts, or discovering contemporary art in boutique shops, visitors are sure to find treasures that encapsulate the essence of this Atlantic gem. The prices are as diverse as the offerings, ensuring that every traveler can bring home a piece of Madeira's unique identity. So, as you plan your visit to this island paradise, be prepared to embark on a shopping adventure that goes beyond acquiring objects – it's a way to connect with the heart and soul of Madeira itself.

9.2 Markets and Shopping Districts

Madeira invites visitors to embark on a unique shopping journey through its vibrant markets and charming shopping districts. From the bustling energy of Funchal's central markets to the quaint boutiques nestled in historic streets, Madeira offers a diverse and immersive shopping experience that captures the essence of the island's culture and hospitality.

Mercado dos Lavradores: Funchal's Iconic Farmers' Market

No exploration of Madeira's markets is complete without a visit to Mercado dos Lavradores, the iconic Farmers' Market located in the heart of Funchal. Here, the air is alive with the vibrant colors and aromas of fresh produce, local crafts, and traditional delicacies. Visitors can stroll through the market's lively stalls, interact with friendly vendors, and discover a vast array of fruits, vegetables, flowers, and handmade crafts. The market, open daily, is a kaleidoscope of flavors, providing an authentic glimpse into Madeira's agricultural and artisanal heritage.

Avenida Arriaga: Funchal's Shopping Boulevard

For those seeking a more modern and cosmopolitan shopping experience, Avenida Arriaga in Funchal is the place to be. This picturesque boulevard, lined with shops, cafes, and restaurants, offers a relaxed atmosphere for leisurely strolls and boutique browsing. Visitors can explore a variety of stores, from international brands to local boutiques, and find everything from fashion and accessories to souvenirs and contemporary art. The avenue comes alive in the evenings, making it an ideal spot for both daytime shopping and nighttime entertainment.

Zona Velha: Historic Charm and Artisanal Treasures

Zona Velha, the historic old town of Funchal, is a charming district that beckons with cobbled streets, colorful buildings, and an eclectic mix of shops. This area is a haven for those seeking unique and artisanal treasures. Boutiques showcase locally crafted items, including traditional embroidery, wickerwork, and handmade jewelry. Visitors can explore the narrow alleys, stumbling upon hidden gems in the form of boutique shops and cozy cafes. Zona Velha is not just a shopping district; it's a step back in time, where history, culture, and commerce converge.

Funchal Design Centre: Contemporary Craftsmanship

For those interested in contemporary craftsmanship and innovative design, the Funchal Design Centre is a must-visit destination. Located in the historic Forte de São Tiago, this center showcases the work of local artists and designers, offering a curated collection of contemporary art, furniture, and unique souvenirs. The center serves as a platform for creative expression, allowing visitors to engage with the cutting-edge design scene on the island.

Forum Madeira: Retail Therapy with Ocean Views

Situated on the outskirts of Funchal, Forum Madeira is a modern shopping mall that combines retail therapy with stunning ocean views. The mall features a diverse range of shops, including fashion outlets, electronics stores, and international brands. With its spacious layout and open-air design, Forum Madeira provides a relaxed and enjoyable shopping experience. Visitors can take a break from shopping to enjoy a meal at one of the mall's restaurants or cafes, all while taking in panoramic views of the Atlantic Ocean.

Exploring Madeira's markets and shopping districts is not just a retail excursion but a journey through the island's diverse cultural landscape. From the traditional charm of Mercado dos Lavradores to the contemporary allure of Avenida Arriaga and the artisanal treasures hidden in Zona Velha, Madeira's shopping tapestry is rich and multifaceted. Whether seeking fresh produce, traditional crafts, or modern design, visitors are sure to find a shopping experience that resonates with the warmth and authenticity of this Atlantic gem. So, as you plan your visit to Madeira, be ready to discover not just souvenirs and gifts but the stories, flavors, and artistic expressions that make shopping on this island a truly unforgettable experience.

9.3 Specialty Stores

Madeira beckons visitors not only with its natural wonders but also with a myriad of specialty stores that offer a unique shopping experience. These establishments, each with its distinctive charm, provide a glimpse into the island's craftsmanship, culinary delights, and artistic expressions.

Bordal – Madeira Embroidery Factory: Where Threads Weave Tales

Located in the heart of Funchal, Bordal is a renowned Madeiran embroidery atelier that seamlessly blends tradition and modern design. This specialty store is a treasure trove for those seeking exquisitely crafted embroidered pieces. Visitors can witness skilled artisans at work, creating intricate patterns on linens, clothing, and accessories. The atelier not only offers a vast selection of embroidered items for purchase but also provides an opportunity to understand the artistry behind Madeira's iconic embroidery.

Cestaria J. Fernandes: Wicker Wonders in Camacha

Nestled in the village of Camacha, Cestaria J. Fernandes is a haven for lovers of traditional wickerwork. This specialty store showcases the craftsmanship of local artisans who skillfully weave wicker into a variety of functional and artistic pieces. From classic baskets to contemporary designs, visitors can explore an extensive collection of wicker wonders. The store's location in the heart of Camacha, known as the "basketwork village," adds an extra layer of authenticity to the shopping experience.

Olaria de São Vicente: Unearth the Art of Ceramics

In São Vicente, the Olaria de São Vicente is a haven for those enamored with handmade ceramics. This specialty store is a testament to the island's rich pottery tradition, offering visitors a chance to peruse an array of unique ceramics, including plates, tiles, and decorative items. Artisans in the workshop showcase their skills, adding a personal touch to each piece. The store not only provides an opportunity to purchase distinctive ceramics but also to gain insights into the time-honored craft of pottery on Madeira.

Armazém do Mercado: A Culinary Expedition in Funchal

Situated within the Mercado dos Lavradores in Funchal, Armazém do Mercado is a culinary haven for those seeking authentic Madeiran flavors. This specialty store is a sensory delight, featuring a curated selection of local produce, wines, and traditional delicacies. Visitors can explore shelves filled with regional specialties, including Madeira wine, honey cakes, and exotic fruits. The knowledgeable staff is ready to offer insights into the island's gastronomic treasures, making this store a must-visit for culinary enthusiasts.

Funchal Design Centre: Contemporary Artistry in Forte de São Tiago

For those inclined towards contemporary art and design, the Funchal Design Centre, located in the historic Forte de São Tiago, is a destination that captivates the imagination. This specialty store showcases a curated collection of contemporary art, furniture, and unique souvenirs created by local artists and designers. Visitors can explore the cutting-edge design scene on the island, taking home pieces that represent the intersection of tradition and innovation.

In essence, exploring the specialty stores of Madeira is an immersive journey that goes beyond traditional shopping. Whether you are drawn to the intricate threads of embroidery at Bordal, the timeless craftsmanship of wicker at Cestaria J. Fernandes, the artistic expressions in ceramics at Olaria de São Vicente, the culinary delights at Armazém do Mercado, or the contemporary artistry at Funchal Design Centre, each specialty store weaves a unique narrative of Madeira's cultural identity. As you plan your visit to this Atlantic gem, let the allure of these specialty stores guide you through a tapestry of specialties, where every purchase becomes a cherished piece of the island's rich heritage.

9.4 Fashion and Design

Madeira not only captivates visitors with its natural beauty but also beckons those with an eye for fashion and design. The island's vibrant fashion scene, blending contemporary styles with traditional craftsmanship, offers a unique shopping experience that reflects the dynamic cultural tapestry of Madeira.

Funchal: The Stylish Heart of Madeira

As the capital and cultural hub of Madeira, Funchal is a haven for fashion enthusiasts. The city's streets are adorned with boutiques and shops that showcase a blend of international trends and local designs. Rua de Santa Maria, the oldest street in Funchal, is a charming thoroughfare dotted with stylish boutiques, presenting an eclectic mix of clothing, accessories, and handmade jewelry. From upscale fashion houses to independent designers, Funchal invites visitors to explore its stylish corners and discover the island's unique sense of style.

Madeiran Embroidery in Fashion: A Timeless Art Form

Madeira is renowned for its intricate embroidery, and this centuries-old craft has found a place in contemporary fashion. Local designers often incorporate traditional embroidery techniques into modern garments, creating pieces that seamlessly bridge the gap between heritage and innovation. Visitors can find exquisite embroidered details on dresses, blouses, and accessories, transforming these items into wearable works of art that capture the essence of Madeira's cultural identity.

Bespoke Fashion and Tailoring: Craftsmanship at its Finest

For those seeking personalized and bespoke fashion experiences, Madeira offers a selection of skilled tailors and ateliers. These craftsmen, often found in the heart of Funchal, bring to life the vision of each individual, creating tailored garments that showcase the artistry of Madeiran tailoring. The process involves meticulous attention to detail, ensuring that visitors leave with not just a piece of clothing but a uniquely crafted expression of their style.

Wicker Fashion in Camacha: Nature-Inspired Elegance

Camacha, known as the "basketwork village," is a hotspot for those looking to explore wicker fashion. Skilled artisans in this village create innovative and stylish pieces using traditional wicker techniques. From handbags to hats, these unique accessories showcase the versatility of wicker as a material. Visitors can not only shop for these distinctive items but also witness the craftsmanship firsthand, gaining an appreciation for the dedication and skill that goes into creating each piece.

Contemporary Art in Wearable Form: Funchal Design Centre

The Funchal Design Centre, located in the historic Forte de São Tiago, is a haven for those interested in wearable art and avant-garde fashion. This center serves as a platform for local designers and artists, showcasing a collection that blurs the lines between fashion and contemporary art. Visitors can explore unique clothing pieces, accessories, and avant-garde designs that reflect the island's creative spirit. The center's gallery-style approach to fashion makes it a destination for those seeking cutting-edge and thought-provoking styles.

Local Boutiques: Discovering Hidden Gems

In addition to the well-known fashion districts, Madeira's local boutiques scattered throughout the island provide hidden gems waiting to be discovered. These smaller establishments often feature handmade items, locally designed clothing, and accessories that capture the essence of Madeira's artistic scene. Exploring these boutiques offers a more intimate and personal shopping experience, allowing visitors to connect with the island's designers on a deeper level.

Exploring fashion and design in Madeira is not just a shopping spree; it's a journey through the island's evolving style narrative. Whether strolling through the chic streets of Funchal, discovering the elegance of wicker fashion in Camacha, or immersing oneself in the avant-garde creations of the Funchal Design Centre, Madeira invites visitors to embrace its unique blend of tradition and innovation. As you plan your visit to this stylish island retreat, prepare to indulge in a fashion experience that not only complements your wardrobe but also weaves the stories and creativity of Madeira into the fabric of your personal style.

9.5 Tips for Bargain Hunting

Madeira, with its diverse markets, boutiques, and specialty stores, presents a unique opportunity for visitors to indulge in the art of bargain hunting. Whether exploring vibrant markets or charming boutiques, the island offers a wealth of treasures waiting to be discovered at favorable prices. Here's a guide to mastering the art of bargain hunting in Madeira and making the most of your shopping experience.

Embrace the Market Culture: Mercado dos Lavradores and Beyond

Mercado dos Lavradores, Funchal's renowned Farmers' Market, is a bustling hub where vibrant colors and lively sounds entice visitors to explore its myriad stalls. Bargain hunting at markets like this is an immersive experience. Engage with local vendors, express genuine interest, and don't hesitate to negotiate prices, especially when purchasing multiple items. Beyond Funchal, explore local markets in smaller towns, where you may find equally charming stalls and more opportunities for bargaining.

Timing Matters: Early Birds and Late Afternoons

Timing is crucial when it comes to bargain hunting in Madeira. Early mornings are ideal for those seeking the freshest produce at markets, and vendors may be more willing to negotiate to kickstart their day. Conversely, late afternoons can also be advantageous, especially towards closing time, when sellers may be more inclined to offer discounts to clear their remaining stock.

Explore Off-the-Beaten-Path Boutiques: Zona Velha and Hidden Gems

While Funchal's main shopping districts offer a plethora of choices, don't overlook the hidden gems in places like Zona Velha, the historic old town. Here, boutique owners may be open to negotiations, providing a more personalized and intimate shopping experience. Explore the less-trodden paths, and you might stumble upon unique boutiques with locally crafted items where bargaining becomes part of the shopping ritual.

Politeness Goes a Long Way: Engage with Locals

In Madeira, politeness and friendliness are cultural norms. Engage with local shopkeepers, ask about the origin of products, and show genuine interest. Establishing a rapport can lead to a more positive shopping experience and may increase the likelihood of receiving a discount. Remember, bargaining is a two-way street, and a respectful approach is key to successful negotiations.

Bundle Your Purchases: The Power of Multiples

When shopping in Madeira, consider bundling your purchases. This tactic can be especially effective in markets where vendors appreciate bulk transactions. Negotiate a comprehensive price for multiple items, and you might find yourself securing a better deal overall. This strategy not only benefits your wallet but also allows you to bring home a collection of diverse Madeiran treasures.

Learn a Few Portuguese Phrases: Bridging the Language Gap

While English is widely spoken, making an effort to learn a few Portuguese phrases can enhance your bargaining experience. Locals appreciate visitors who make an attempt to speak their language, even if it's just a few basic expressions. This cultural gesture may contribute to a more amicable negotiation process, fostering a connection between you and the sellers.

Consider Cash Payments: Cash is King in Bargaining

In many smaller establishments, cash payments are preferred and might even work in your favor during negotiations. Shopkeepers may be more willing to offer discounts when transactions are settled in cash, as it eliminates credit card processing fees. Before embarking on your shopping adventure, ensure you have enough local currency on hand to take advantage of potential cash discounts.

Stay Open-Minded: Unearth Unexpected Finds

Bargain hunting in Madeira is not just about scoring low prices; it's also about unearthing unexpected finds. Be open-minded and willing to explore hidden corners, whether in markets, boutiques, or local artisan workshops. The thrill of discovering a unique, handcrafted item at a favorable price adds an extra layer of satisfaction to your shopping experience.

In conclusion, mastering the art of bargain hunting in Madeira is a skill that adds excitement and cultural immersion to your shopping endeavors. From the vibrant markets to the quaint boutiques, the island provides a canvas for savvy shoppers to explore, negotiate, and uncover treasures. As you plan your visit to this shopper's paradise, relish the opportunity to engage with local vendors, embrace the market culture, and let the art of bargaining become a memorable part of your Madeiran adventure.

CHAPTER 10

DAY TRIPS AND EXCURSIONS

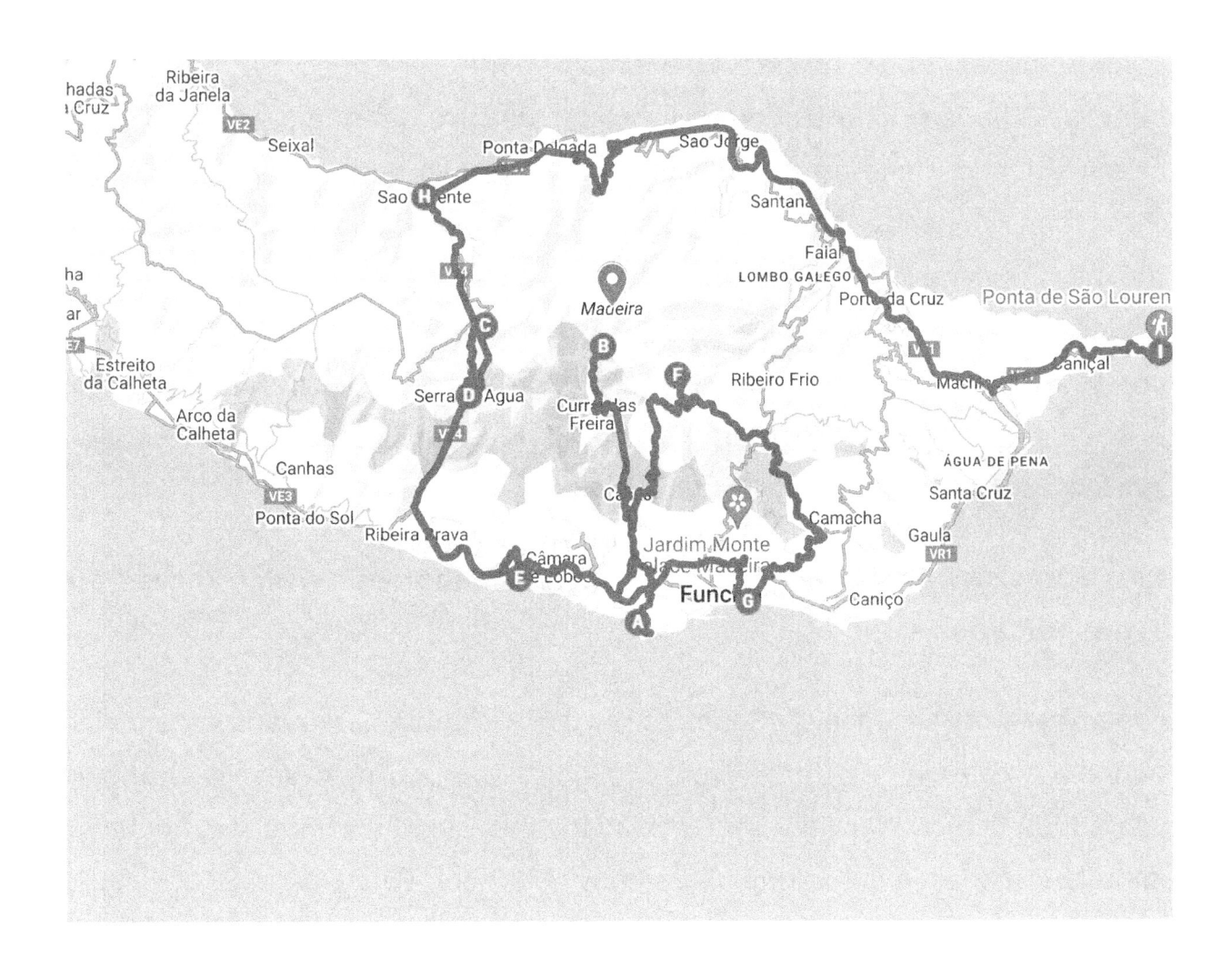

10.1 Nearby Islands

Embarking on day trips and excursions to nearby islands from Madeira is an enticing prospect for travelers seeking to expand their Atlantic horizons. The archipelago's strategic location allows for easy exploration of neighboring gems, each with its unique charm and allure. Let's delve into the possibilities that await adventurous visitors keen on discovering the wonders just beyond Madeira's shores.

The Enchanting Porto Santo: A Day in Paradise with Affordable Transportation Cost

A mere ferry ride or a short flight from Madeira transports visitors to the golden shores of Porto Santo, a small island renowned for its pristine beaches. The ferry journey itself is a scenic delight, offering panoramic views of the Atlantic. Once on Porto Santo, travelers can bask in the sunshine on the expansive sandy beaches, known for their therapeutic properties due to the high mineral content of the sand. The island's relaxed pace, charming villages, and historical sites, including the Christopher Columbus House, create a serene day-long escape. Ferry tickets are available at reasonable prices, providing an economical option for day-trippers. Flights are also available for those seeking a quicker journey.

La Gomera: A Green Oasis in the Canaries with Accessible Transportation Cost

For a taste of the Spanish Canaries, a day trip to La Gomera is an enticing option. Accessible by ferry from Funchal, the journey unveils stunning seascapes before reaching San Sebastián, the island's capital. La Gomera's lush landscapes and unique Garajonay National Park, a UNESCO World Heritage site, offer a contrasting experience to Madeira. Visitors can explore dense laurel forests, discover picturesque villages, and indulge in local cuisine. The island's distinct whistling language, Silbo Gomero, adds a cultural charm to this immersive day-trip experience. Ferry tickets to La Gomera are reasonably priced, making it an accessible option for day-trippers.

São Miguel in the Azores: A Tropical Paradise in the North Atlantic with Worthwhile Transportation Cost

Venturing farther into the North Atlantic, a day trip to São Miguel, the largest island in the Azores archipelago, is an adventurous possibility for those seeking a diverse natural landscape. A short flight from Madeira transports visitors to São Miguel's lush scenery, volcanic craters, and natural hot springs. The town of Furnas is renowned for its geothermal activity, offering a unique chance to bathe in naturally heated thermal pools. The island's Blue and Green Lakes, set amidst verdant landscapes, add a touch of surreal beauty to this day-long Azorean escapade. Flights to São Miguel are available, and though slightly more expensive, the journey is well worth the immersive experience the Azores offer.

Practical Considerations: Planning Your Island Adventure

Before embarking on day trips to nearby islands, travelers should consider practical aspects for a seamless experience. Checking ferry or flight schedules, making advance reservations, and being aware of visa requirements (if applicable) are essential. It's advisable to plan the day's itinerary in advance to make the most of the limited time on the destination island.

Day trips and excursions to nearby islands from Madeira present a realm of island-hopping possibilities, each offering a unique escape from the familiar shores of the archipelago. From the golden beaches of Porto Santo to the lush landscapes of La Gomera and the volcanic wonders of São Miguel, these day trips add layers to the rich tapestry of experiences for adventurous visitors. The affordability of transportation options ensures that island-hopping dreams can come true for those eager to explore beyond Madeira's captivating horizons.

10.2 Scenic Drives

Madeira, an island gem in the Atlantic, invites visitors to embark on unforgettable scenic drives that unveil the breathtaking beauty of its landscapes. With winding roads that traverse lush mountains, dramatic cliffs, and picturesque coastal stretches, the scenic drives in Madeira promise an immersive journey through nature's masterpiece.

The Famous Estrada Monumental: Funchal's Coastal Marvel

Begin your scenic exploration in Funchal with a drive along the famous Estrada Monumental. This coastal road offers stunning views of the Atlantic Ocean on one side and the vibrant cityscape of Funchal on the other. Lined with palm trees, gardens, and charming cafes, it provides the perfect introduction to the natural and architectural wonders that define Madeira.

Curves of Encumeada: A Mountainous Odyssey

For those seeking a mountainous adventure, the drive to Encumeada is a must. The road winds its way through the central mountains, revealing panoramic vistas of valleys and peaks. As you ascend, the landscape transforms, showcasing the island's diverse ecosystems. The viewpoint at Encumeada offers a captivating panorama where the North and South coasts merge, providing a breathtaking snapshot of Madeira's geographical diversity.

Serra de Água: Valley Serenity and Rugged Peaks

Continue your scenic journey to Serra de Água, a picturesque valley nestled between towering peaks. The drive through this region is a serene experience, surrounded by terraced vineyards and quaint villages. The imposing rock formations and rugged cliffs create a dramatic backdrop, making Serra de Água a captivating destination for those seeking both tranquility and awe-inspiring landscapes.

The Spectacular Cabo Girão: Europe's Highest Cliff Skywalk

As your exploration continues, venture towards Cabo Girão, a natural wonder that boasts Europe's highest cliff skywalk. The drive leading to Cabo Girão treats visitors to awe-inspiring coastal panoramas. Once there, step onto the glass-floored skywalk for a thrilling experience, providing a vertiginous view of the cliffs, the ocean below, and the charming coastal villages.

Pico do Arieiro to Pico Ruivo: A High Altitude Expedition

For an elevated adventure, take the scenic drive from Pico do Arieiro to Pico Ruivo, the highest peak in Madeira. The journey unfolds through the clouds, revealing a surreal landscape of jagged peaks and alpine vegetation. The road is a gateway to hiking trails that lead to Pico Ruivo's summit, offering panoramic views that make the journey truly worthwhile.

Through Laurissilva Forests: Rabaçal and 25 Fontes

Explore the mystical Laurissilva Forests with a drive to Rabaçal, a gateway to some of Madeira's most enchanting hiking trails. The road leads to the Risco and 25 Fontes waterfalls, where emerald greenery and cascading water create a serene ambiance. The drive itself is a journey through laurel-scented air, immersing visitors in the ancient beauty of these UNESCO-listed forests.

Practical Tips for Scenic Drives in Madeira: Navigating the Island's Terrain

While navigating the scenic drives in Madeira, it's essential to consider the island's unique terrain. Roads can be narrow and winding, with steep ascents and descents. Ensure your vehicle is in good condition, and take your time to savor each panoramic view safely. Consider renting a car with a panoramic roof for an enhanced visual experience.

The scenic drives of Madeira offer a captivating road trip through a landscape of unparalleled beauty. From coastal roads and mountainous passes to lush valleys and ancient forests, each drive presents a new facet of the island's natural splendor. As you navigate the winding roads and explore the diverse landscapes, the scenic drives of Madeira promise not only breathtaking views but also an immersive journey into the heart of this Atlantic paradise. So, buckle up, embark on a road trip adventure, and let the scenic drives of Madeira become an indelible part of your travel story.

10.3 Historical Day Trips

Embarking on historical day trips from Madeira is a captivating exploration that allows visitors to traverse centuries and uncover the rich tapestry of the island's past. These excursions offer a delightful blend of architectural wonders, cultural heritage, and tales of bygone eras, all within a day's reach from the vibrant shores of Madeira.

Funchal's Old Town and Historic Landmarks: A Walk Through Time

Begin your historical voyage in Funchal, the heart of Madeira, where the Old Town stands as a living testament to the island's colonial history. Stroll through cobbled streets lined with colorful houses adorned with wrought-iron balconies. Visit the Sé Cathedral, a Gothic masterpiece dating back to the 15th century, and discover the charm of the Santa Clara Convent, showcasing Mudejar architecture. The Mercado dos Lavradores, a bustling market since the 1930s, provides a sensory feast of local flavors and artisanal crafts. Exploring Funchal's historical gems is conveniently done on foot, allowing for an immersive experience at no additional transportation cost.

São Vicente: Tracing Madeira's Volcanic Origins

Venture northwest to São Vicente, a village nestled between towering cliffs and the Atlantic Ocean, offering a glimpse into Madeira's volcanic origins. The São Vicente Caves and Volcanism Centre provide an educational journey underground, where visitors can explore lava tunnels and learn about the island's geological evolution. The quaint village itself, with its 17th-century church and traditional houses, adds a charming historical touch to the day trip. Public buses or rental cars are viable options for reaching São Vicente, with affordable fares for a day trip.

Ponta de São Lourenço: Coastal Exploration and Fortress History

Embark on an excursion to Ponta de São Lourenço, the easternmost point of Madeira, where dramatic cliffs meet the Atlantic. The coastal walk reveals stunning vistas and geological formations shaped by wind and waves. At the tip of the peninsula, Forte de São Lourenço, a 17th-century fortress, stands as a sentinel overlooking the sea. Explore the fortress to delve into Madeira's defensive history and savor panoramic views of the coastline. Buses or rental cars provide access to Ponta de São Lourenço, offering flexibility for a day trip.

Machico and the Legacy of the Discoverers: Exploring Early Expeditions

Head to Machico, Madeira's second-oldest town, to delve into the island's maritime history and the legacy of its early discoverers. The golden sands of Machico Beach mark the spot where Portuguese explorers, including João Gonçalves Zarco, first landed in 1419. Visit the Capela dos Milagres, a 15th-century chapel, and the Fort of São João Baptista, built to protect the town from pirates. The town's picturesque charm, steeped in maritime heritage, invites visitors to step back in time. Public buses or rental cars provide access to Machico, offering an affordable means for a historical day trip.

Practical Considerations: Crafting Your Historical Exploration

When planning historical day trips from Madeira, consider practical aspects to ensure a seamless and enriching experience. Checking opening hours of historical sites, considering guided tours for in-depth insights, and choosing suitable transportation options contribute to a well-rounded exploration.

Historical day trips from Madeira offer a fascinating journey through time, allowing visitors to uncover the island's timeless treasures. From the historic charm of Funchal's Old Town to the geological wonders of São Vicente, the coastal exploration of Ponta de São Lourenço, and the maritime legacy in Machico, each excursion unveils a unique facet of Madeira's rich history. As you embark on these historical adventures, the past comes alive, weaving a narrative that connects the present to the island's enduring legacy.

10.4 Adventure Day Excursions

Madeira, a picturesque jewel in the Atlantic Ocean, invites adventurers to experience the island's natural wonders through a series of exhilarating day excursions. From the rugged mountains to the azure coastline, these adventures promise an unforgettable journey into the heart of Madeira's breathtaking landscapes. As you plan your escape into the realm of excitement, consider the following insights into transportation costs, expectations, and essential information for each thrilling adventure.

Cost of Transportation: Navigating the Island's Beauty

The journey into the heart of Madeira's adventure begins with the consideration of transportation. Various tour operators on the island offer packages inclusive of transportation from accommodations. Prices vary based on the chosen adventure, encompassing a range from moderate to higher-end options. Prospective adventurers are encouraged to check with local tour providers for the most up-to-date pricing.

Levada Walks: Tranquil Hikes in Nature's Embrace

For those craving a blend of adventure and tranquility, Levada walks beckon. These irrigation channels, adorned by lush greenery, form a network of hiking trails across the island. Guided tours are available, ensuring not just a hike but an educational journey through Madeira's flora and fauna. Participants can expect breathtaking views of valleys, waterfalls, and pristine landscapes, all while savoring the soothing sounds of nature.

Canyoning in Ribeira das Cales: Descending Nature's Waterslides

Ribeira das Cales introduces adventurers to the thrill of canyoning, a blend of hiking, swimming, and rappelling down waterfalls in the island's rugged landscapes. This adrenaline-pumping activity promises encounters with nature's waterslides and rocky formations, creating an unforgettable and immersive experience. The cost of canyoning excursions varies, offering moderate to high-end options, reflective of the specialized equipment and guides required.

Jeep Safaris to São Vicente: Off-Road Exploration Unveiled

For those with a penchant for off-road exploration, Jeep safaris to São Vicente provide an exhilarating journey through Madeira's rugged interior. These excursions venture off the beaten path, navigating mountainous terrain, dense forests, and picturesque valleys. Adventurers can anticipate panoramic views and the discovery of hidden gems inaccessible by traditional transportation. The cost of Jeep safaris falls within a moderate to high range, considering the specialized vehicles and experienced guides provided.

Dolphin and Whale Watching: Maritime Serenity Unveiled

Maritime enthusiasts can embark on dolphin and whale-watching excursions, setting sail from coastal towns like Funchal. The Atlantic waters surrounding Madeira are home to a variety of marine life, offering participants the chance to witness dolphins, whales, and other sea creatures in their natural habitat. The moderate cost of these tours makes it an accessible option for those looking to explore Madeira's marine wonders.

Paragliding in Arco da Calheta: Soaring Above Coastal Beauty

For the ultimate aerial adventure, paragliding in Arco da Calheta provides a unique perspective of Madeira's stunning coastline. Guided by experienced instructors, participants can soar through the skies, marveling at panoramic views of the Atlantic Ocean, cliffs, and charming coastal villages below. While paragliding experiences tend to be on the higher end of the cost spectrum, the thrill of soaring above the picturesque landscapes makes it a worthwhile investment for adventure seekers.

Practical Tips for Adventure Day Excursions: Safely Navigating Madeira's Terrain

As adventurers prepare for their day excursions, practical considerations enhance the overall experience. Madeira's terrain, characterized by narrow and winding roads, steep ascents, and descents, demands attention to safety. Ensuring the chosen vehicle is in good condition becomes imperative, and participants are advised to take their time, relishing each panoramic view responsibly. Renting a car with a panoramic roof can enhance the visual experience, adding an extra layer of enjoyment to the adventure.

The adventure day excursions from Madeira offer a spectrum of experiences that cater to diverse tastes. Whether hiking along levadas, canyoning in Ribeira das Cales, embarking on Jeep safaris to São Vicente, witnessing marine life through dolphin and whale-watching, or soaring above coastal beauty in Arco da Calheta, each adventure promises a unique and memorable experience. As travelers plan their visit to Madeira, the opportunity to blend adrenaline-pumping activities with the island's natural beauty becomes a defining feature of their itinerary, creating moments that linger in memory long after the adventure concludes.

10.5 Relaxing Getaways

Madeira not only offers adventurous pursuits but also serves as a gateway to serene retreats. These relaxing getaways, scattered across the archipelago, beckon visitors seeking tranquility and rejuvenation. Let's explore the idyllic escapes that provide a perfect balance to the vibrant energy of Madeira.

Porto Santo: The Golden Haven

A short ferry or flight transports travelers to the golden shores of Porto Santo, an island basking in tranquility. Known for its therapeutic sands, visitors can indulge in a day of blissful relaxation on the extensive sandy beaches. The calming rhythm of the ocean and the island's laid-back ambiance create a haven for those seeking respite. Luxurious resorts offer spa treatments, and seaside cafes provide the perfect setting for unwinding with a view of the endless horizon. Consider booking accommodation with beachfront access to maximize your relaxation time.

Santana: A Rural Oasis Amidst Laurel Forests

For a retreat immersed in nature, head to Santana, a village surrounded by lush laurel forests and verdant landscapes. Quaint cottages known as "palheiros" offer a unique accommodation experience, allowing guests to wake up to the soothing sounds of nature. Take leisurely walks through the forest trails, breathe in the fresh mountain air, and immerse yourself in the tranquility of this rural oasis. The traditional Santana houses provide a charming backdrop for a stress-free escape. Check for eco-friendly accommodations that align with the natural beauty of the surroundings.

Seixal: Coastal Serenity and Natural Pools

Nestled along the northern coast, Seixal offers a picturesque retreat with its black sand beaches and natural rock pools. The soothing sound of waves crashing against the volcanic shores creates a melody for relaxation. Visitors can bask in the sun, take a dip in the natural pools, and enjoy breathtaking views of the Atlantic. Seixal provides an off-the-beaten-path escape, allowing guests to unwind amidst the untouched beauty of Madeira's coastal serenity. Bring sunscreen, a good book, and a picnic for a leisurely day by the natural pools.

Calheta: Blissful Beach Retreats

Calheta, with its golden sandy beaches and calm waters, offers a blissful beach retreat on the southwest coast of Madeira. Surrounded by rolling hills and banana plantations, the town exudes a tranquil charm. Resorts and boutique hotels line the coastline, providing a perfect setting for a relaxing escape. Visitors can enjoy leisurely walks along the beach, partake in water activities, or simply unwind by the shores with the gentle sea breeze as their companion. Explore local seafood restaurants for a taste of Madeiran culinary delights.

São Vicente: Cliffside Serenity and Laurissilva Forest

São Vicente, embraced by dramatic cliffs and the soothing embrace of Laurissilva Forest, offers a serene retreat for nature lovers. Tranquil walks through the laurel forest provide a meditative experience, while the cliffs provide stunning panoramic views of the Atlantic. Visitors can find solace in the quietude of this coastal town, away from the bustle of city life. The sound of the forest, the rustling leaves, and the distant ocean waves create a symphony of relaxation. Pack comfortable walking shoes for exploring the forest trails and cliffside viewpoints.

Practical Considerations: Crafting Your Relaxing Retreat

When planning a relaxing getaway from Madeira, consider practical aspects to ensure a stress-free experience. Check for wellness services offered at accommodations, inquire about nature excursions, and pack accordingly for the type of retreat you desire.

The relaxing getaways from Madeira offer an array of experiences, from golden beaches to forested hillsides and coastal cliffs. These retreats provide a tranquil escape, allowing visitors to rejuvenate amidst nature's embrace. Whether you seek the therapeutic sands of Porto Santo or the quietude of São Vicente's laurel forest, each destination invites you to unwind, creating a harmonious balance to the exhilarating adventures awaiting on Madeira's main island.

CHAPTER 11

ENTERTAINMENT AND NIGHTLIFE

11.1 Bars and Pubs

As the sun sets over the Atlantic, Madeira comes alive with a vibrant nightlife, offering a variety of bars and pubs that cater to diverse tastes. These establishments, each with its unique ambiance and character, provide visitors with a delightful array of options to unwind and embrace the lively spirit of the island.

Café do Teatro: Funchal's Artistic Hub: Nestled in the heart of Funchal, Café do Teatro stands as an artistic haven. Located near the Teatro Municipal Baltazar Dias, this bar exudes a bohemian charm, attracting both locals and tourists alike. The interior, adorned with vintage furnishings and local artwork, creates an intimate setting. Open until the early hours, Café do Teatro hosts live music performances, poetry readings, and art exhibitions. Prices are moderate, offering a selection of local wines, craft beers, and creative cocktails.

The Hole in One Pub: Golf-Themed Relaxation

For those seeking a unique pub experience, The Hole in One Pub in Funchal delivers a golf-themed ambiance that stands out. Located near the marina, this pub boasts a cozy interior adorned with golf memorabilia. Patrons can enjoy a range of international and local beers, including Madeira's craft beer offerings. Prices are reasonable, making it a popular spot for locals and golf enthusiasts. The pub opens in the late afternoon and extends its warm hospitality until the late evening.

Moynihan's Irish Bar: Authentic Irish Flair

For a taste of Ireland in the heart of Madeira, Moynihan's Irish Bar in Funchal provides an authentic pub experience. Situated in the old town area, this welcoming establishment is known for its Irish hospitality, live music, and a diverse selection of Irish whiskies and beers. Prices are moderate, and the pub opens in the early evening, making it an ideal spot for those looking to start their night with a relaxed atmosphere and a touch of Celtic charm.

The Beerhouse: Craft Beer Extravaganza

In the charming town of Ponta do Sol, The Beerhouse stands as a haven for craft beer enthusiasts. This cozy establishment, tucked away in a traditional Madeiran building, offers an extensive menu of local and international craft beers. The ambiance is laid-back, with outdoor seating available for those who wish to enjoy their drinks under the stars. Prices vary based on the beer selection, ensuring there's an option for every budget. The Beerhouse opens in the early evening and provides a casual setting for beer aficionados.

The Ritz Madeira: Oceanfront Elegance

For those yearning for a touch of sophistication and an oceanfront view, The Ritz Madeira, located in Caniço, is a premier cocktail lounge. As part of a luxury resort, this establishment provides an elegant setting for patrons to indulge in expertly crafted cocktails and premium spirits. The terrace overlooks the Atlantic, creating a romantic ambiance. Prices reflect the upscale nature of the venue, making it an ideal location for a special night out. The Ritz Madeira opens in the evening, offering a refined atmosphere for those seeking a more elevated nightlife experience.

Practical Considerations: Planning Your Night Out

When exploring bars and pubs in Madeira, consider practical aspects to enhance your experience. Check for special events or live performances, inquire about happy hour deals, and be mindful of the closing hours, as some establishments may close earlier during weekdays.

The bars and pubs of Madeira offer a diverse tapestry of experiences, from artistic and bohemian vibes to authentic Irish charm, craft beer havens, and upscale cocktail lounges. Whether you're sipping a craft beer at The Beerhouse, enjoying live music at Café do Teatro, or relishing premium cocktails at The Ritz Madeira, each venue contributes to the vibrant nightlife of this Atlantic gem. As you traverse the bars and pubs of Madeira, you're sure to find a night to remember, filled with unique flavors, lively atmospheres, and the warm hospitality for which the island is renowned.

11.2 Nightclubs

As the sun dips below the horizon, Madeira's nightlife continues to flourish, beckoning night owls to its array of pulsating nightclubs. These hotspots, each with its unique energy and allure, create an unforgettable nocturnal experience. Let's delve into the vibrant world of Madeira's nightclubs, where the beats are contagious, and the ambiance electrifying.

F Club: Funchal's Dance Haven

Located in the heart of Funchal, F Club stands as a pulsating dance haven for those seeking an immersive nightclub experience. With a modern interior and cutting-edge sound system, F Club attracts both locals and visitors looking to dance the night away. The club opens its doors late into the evening and stays alive until the early morning hours. Prices for entry and drinks are reasonable, making it an accessible destination for a lively night out. The DJ lineup often features both local talents and international acts, ensuring a diverse and energetic music selection.

Vespas Club: A Retro Escape in Machico

For a unique throwback experience, Vespas Club in Machico offers a retro ambiance that stands out. Nestled in the historic town, this nightclub is known for its vintage décor, including classic Vespas displayed throughout the venue. The music playlist spans across the decades, creating a nostalgic atmosphere that resonates with patrons. Prices for drinks are reasonable, and the club welcomes partygoers until the early morning. Vespas Club's unique blend of retro vibes and contemporary beats provides a distinct nightlife experience on Madeira.

Copacabana Club: Tropical Vibes in Funchal

Transporting visitors to a tropical paradise, Copacabana Club in Funchal is a vibrant nightclub with a Brazilian twist. Located near the marina, the club features lively Latin rhythms, creating an energetic dance floor. The décor embraces a carnival spirit, complete with colorful lights and festive accents. Copacabana Club opens late into the night, ensuring a lively atmosphere until the early hours. Prices are moderate, offering an affordable option for those looking to revel in tropical vibes while sipping on exotic cocktails.

Voodoo Club: Electronic Beats in Lido

For enthusiasts of electronic music, Voodoo Club in the Lido area of Funchal provides a dynamic space to dance to the beats of renowned DJs. The club's sleek and modern design, coupled with state-of-the-art lighting, enhances the overall experience. Voodoo Club opens its doors late into the evening and keeps the energy alive until dawn. While the electronic scene takes center stage, the club occasionally hosts themed nights to diversify the musical offerings. Prices for entry and drinks align with the energetic atmosphere, providing an exhilarating destination for electronic music lovers.

Blues Bar & Disco: A Multi-Faceted Nightlife Experience

Situated in the heart of Ponta do Sol, Blues Bar & Disco offers a multi-faceted nightlife experience, combining a relaxed bar atmosphere with a vibrant dance floor. The venue opens early as a bar, providing a laid-back setting for socializing and enjoying live music. As the night progresses, the atmosphere transforms into a lively disco, inviting patrons to dance until the early morning. Prices are reasonable, catering to both those seeking a chill evening and those ready to hit the dance floor. Blues Bar & Disco's versatility makes it a popular destination for a diverse crowd.

Practical Considerations: Navigating the Nightlife Scene

When venturing into the nightlife scene of Madeira, consider practical aspects to ensure a seamless experience. Check the dress code for specific nightclubs, inquire about special events or themed nights, and be aware of any entry requirements. Most nightclubs have a minimum age requirement, so it's essential to bring a valid ID.

Madeira's nightclubs offer a dynamic spectrum of experiences, from pulsating dance floors to retro throwback vibes and tropical escapades. Whether you find yourself immersed in the beats of F Club, relishing retro nostalgia at Vespas Club, dancing to Latin rhythms in Copacabana Club, enjoying electronic beats in Voodoo Club, or experiencing the multi-faceted ambiance of Blues Bar & Disco, each nightclub contributes to the island's vibrant nightlife. As you explore the rhythmic revelry of Madeira's nightclubs, you're sure to find a nighttime haven that resonates with your desire for energetic beats, diverse atmospheres, and unforgettable moments under the starlit skies.

11.3 Live Music Venues

Madeira's enchanting evenings come alive with the soulful melodies and rhythmic beats of its live music venues. These establishments, each with its unique ambiance and musical offerings, beckon visitors to immerse themselves in the island's vibrant cultural scene. Let's embark on a musical journey through five live music venues that define Madeira's harmonious nights.

Funchal Jazz Club: Intimate Jazz Soirees

Nestled in the heart of Funchal, the Funchal Jazz Club stands as a haven for jazz enthusiasts. Located in the Old Town area, this intimate venue showcases local and international jazz acts in a cozy setting. The entrance fee is reasonable, offering access to an evening of sophisticated jazz performances. The club opens in the late evening, providing a perfect escape for those seeking an atmospheric night filled with smooth jazz melodies. Funchal Jazz Club occasionally hosts jam sessions, creating an interactive experience for both musicians and patrons.

Maktub Pub: Eclectic Vibes in Funchal

For a diverse musical experience, Maktub Pub in Funchal offers an eclectic ambiance where various genres come together. Located near the marina, this lively pub features live bands, solo artists, and themed nights that cater to a range of musical tastes. The entrance fee is typically modest, allowing patrons to enjoy the performances without breaking the bank. Maktub Pub opens its doors in the early evening and extends its musical festivities until the late hours. The venue's laid-back atmosphere and friendly crowd contribute to its charm.

Clube de Jazz do Funchal: A Fusion of Styles

Situated in the São Pedro neighborhood of Funchal, the Clube de Jazz do Funchal is a versatile live music venue that explores a fusion of styles. The entrance fee is reasonable, providing access to an array of performances spanning jazz, blues, and world music. The club opens its doors in the evening, welcoming music enthusiasts to a cozy and intimate space. Clube de Jazz do Funchal occasionally hosts themed nights and collaborations with local artists, adding an element of surprise to each visit.

Sabores do Fado: Fado Nights in Funchal

For a taste of Portugal's soul-stirring fado music, Sabores do Fado in Funchal is a quintessential venue. Located in the historic Old Town, this establishment specializes in fado performances accompanied by traditional Portuguese cuisine. The entrance fee often includes a meal, providing a complete cultural experience. Sabores do Fado opens its doors in the early evening, creating a serene atmosphere for patrons to revel in the heartfelt expressions of fado singers. The venue's authentic ambiance, combined with the emotive sounds of fado, offers a unique and memorable night out.

Pérola Negra: Rock and Roll Vibes in Funchal

For rock enthusiasts, Pérola Negra in Funchal stands as a beacon of the island's rock and roll scene. Located in the Lido area, this vibrant venue hosts live rock bands and themed nights dedicated to the genre. The entrance fee is usually reasonable, attracting a diverse crowd of rock aficionados. Pérola Negra opens its doors late into the evening, providing a lively space for patrons to immerse themselves in the energetic beats of live rock performances. The venue's energetic atmosphere, combined with its dedication to the rock genre, creates an electric experience for music lovers.

Practical Considerations: Planning Your Musical Night Out

When planning a night out at live music venues in Madeira, consider practical aspects to enhance your experience. Check the schedule for featured artists, inquire about any special events or themed nights, and be mindful of the opening and closing hours. Some venues may have age restrictions, so it's advisable to check beforehand.

Madeira's live music venues offer a symphony of sounds, from the smooth jazz melodies at Funchal Jazz Club to the diverse genres at Maktub Pub, the fusion of styles at Clube de Jazz do Funchal, the emotive fado nights at Sabores do Fado, and the energetic rock and roll vibes at Pérola Negra. Each venue contributes to the island's cultural richness, providing visitors with an opportunity to immerse themselves in the diverse musical tapestry of Madeira. As you explore these live music venues, you're sure to discover nights filled with harmony, rhythm, and the warm embrace of Madeira's musical spirit.

11.4 Cultural Performances

From traditional folk dances to melodious fado tunes, the cultural performances in Madeira offer visitors a captivating journey into the heart and soul of this Atlantic gem. Let's embark on an exploration of the diverse and enchanting cultural performances that grace the stages of Madeira.

Folkloric Dances: A Celebration of Heritage

At the heart of Madeira's cultural performances lies a celebration of its rich heritage through folkloric dances. In quaint villages and vibrant town squares, locals clad in colorful traditional costumes twirl and stomp to the rhythm of lively music. These dances, deeply rooted in Madeiran history, showcase the island's agricultural traditions, fishing culture, and the joyous spirit of its people. Whether witnessing the "Bailinho da Madeira" or the energetic "Chamarrita," visitors are transported back in time, experiencing the authenticity of Madeira's cultural tapestry.

Fado Nights: Embracing the Soulful Melodies

For those seeking an emotional journey through music, Fado nights in Madeira provide an intimate encounter with Portugal's soul-stirring musical genre. Venues like Sabores do Fado, nestled in the historic Old Town of Funchal, offer enchanting evenings where fado singers pour their hearts into melancholic and poetic tunes. The soulful melodies echo the tales of love, longing, and saudade, creating an atmosphere that resonates with the deep emotions embedded in Portuguese culture.

Traditional Music: A Symphony of Madeiran Sounds

Beyond folkloric dances and fado, Madeira's cultural performances include a symphony of traditional music, played on instruments that have endured through generations. From the braguinha, a small guitar-like instrument, to the rajão and the brinquinho, these musical pieces reflect the island's diverse influences, blending Portuguese, African, and Moorish elements. Talented musicians, often found in local festivals and events, showcase the versatility of Madeiran traditional music, leaving audiences enchanted by the harmonious blend of strings and percussion.

Carnival Celebrations: A Riot of Colors and Rhythms

Carnival season in Madeira transforms the island into a riot of colors, music, and exuberant cultural performances. The streets come alive with vibrant parades, showcasing elaborate costumes, lively dances, and infectious rhythms. The Carnival of Funchal, one of the island's most renowned celebrations, attracts both locals and tourists with its grand floats, samba rhythms, and the traditional masked characters known as "Tricanas" and "Lavadeiras." The cultural energy during Carnival is palpable, inviting everyone to revel in the vivacity of Madeira's festive spirit.

Traditional Festivals: Commemorating Saints and Seasons

Throughout the year, Madeira hosts a myriad of traditional festivals that blend religious fervor with cultural performances. The Festival of São João, celebrated in Funchal and other towns, is a prime example. It honors the patron saint of the island with processions, music, and traditional games. Similarly, the Festival of São Vicente pays homage to the patron saint of the village, incorporating cultural performances, processions, and a lively street fair. These festivals not only commemorate saints but also serve as vibrant showcases of Madeiran traditions.

The cultural performances in Madeira offer a profound and immersive journey into the island's soul. From the exuberance of folkloric dances to the emotive strains of fado, the island's cultural stage comes alive with authenticity and passion. Traditional music, Carnival celebrations, and festive street processions further contribute to the enchanting tapestry of Madeira's cultural heritage. As you witness these performances, you not only become a spectator but a participant in the vibrant narrative of an island that proudly embraces and shares its cultural richness with the world.

11.5 Festivals and Celebrations

The island of Madeira comes alive with a kaleidoscope of colors, music, and traditions during its vibrant festivals and celebrations. These lively events, deeply rooted in the island's rich cultural tapestry, not only commemorate religious and historical milestones but also serve as a testament to the warmth and exuberance of the Madeiran spirit. Let's embark on a journey through the festive calendar of Madeira, where every celebration is a joyful invitation to join in the island's merriment.

Carnival of Funchal: A Carnival Extravaganza

When February arrives, Madeira transforms into a lively spectacle of music, dance, and elaborate costumes during the Carnival of Funchal. This grand celebration, one of the largest in Europe, captivates locals and visitors alike with its exuberant parades, samba rhythms, and colorful floats. The streets are adorned with vibrant decorations, and the air is filled with the infectious energy of masked revelers and traditional characters. From the whimsical "Tricanas" to the spirited "Lavadeiras," the Carnival of Funchal is a joyous extravaganza that transcends age and background, inviting everyone to partake in the island's festive spirit.

Festival of São João: A Midsummer Night's Celebration

As the warmth of June envelopes the island, Madeira commemorates the Festival of São João, a celebration that blends religious devotion with cultural merriment. In Funchal and other towns, processions wind through the streets, honoring the patron saint with lively music and traditional dances. The night sky comes alive with colorful fireworks, casting a magical glow over the festivities. Traditional games and street fairs add to the jovial atmosphere, making the Festival of São João a delightful showcase of Madeiran traditions.

Madeira Wine Festival: Toasting to Tradition

In September, the Madeira Wine Festival takes center stage, paying homage to the island's renowned wine culture. The festivities kick off with the historical grape harvest parade, where locals dressed in traditional costumes carry baskets of grapes through Funchal's streets. The scent of ripe grapes fills the air as the procession culminates in the symbolic treading of the grapes, a nod to centuries-old winemaking traditions. The festival continues with wine tastings, musical performances, and vibrant street parties, inviting both wine enthusiasts and curious visitors to savor the essence of Madeira's viticultural heritage.

Christmas and New Year's Eve: Luminous Celebrations

As the year draws to a close, Madeira decks itself in sparkling lights and festive decorations, creating a magical ambiance for Christmas and New Year's Eve celebrations. Funchal's streets transform into a luminous spectacle with the famous Christmas lights display, attracting visitors from around the world. The New Year's Eve fireworks extravaganza is a highlight, as the night sky over the bay is illuminated with a breathtaking display, earning Madeira a spot on the list of the world's best New Year's Eve destinations. Locals and tourists gather to welcome the new year with joyous cheers and the vibrant energy that characterizes Madeira's celebratory spirit.

Festival of São Vicente: Honoring the Patron Saint

In the picturesque town of São Vicente, the Festival of São Vicente pays homage to the patron saint through a blend of religious processions and cultural festivities. The charming streets come alive with colorful decorations, and the air resonates with traditional music and dance. The festival creates a communal atmosphere where locals and visitors come together to celebrate the identity and traditions of São Vicente. The festivities often extend to include a lively street fair, creating a sense of camaraderie and joy.

In conclusion, the festivals and celebrations of Madeira paint a vivid portrait of an island that cherishes its traditions and embraces the joy of communal festivities. From the grandeur of the Carnival of Funchal to the cultural richness of the Festival of São João, and the luminous charm of Christmas and New Year's Eve, Madeira offers a year-round symphony of joy. These celebrations not only commemorate historical and religious milestones but also serve as an open invitation for everyone to join in the island's warmth, exuberance, and unwavering sense of community. Whether you find yourself amidst the lively Carnival parades or experiencing the enchantment of a grape harvest, each festival in Madeira is a vibrant thread woven into the tapestry of an island that celebrates life with resounding cheer.

CONCLUSION AND INSIDER TIPS FOR VISITORS

As we draw the curtains on this comprehensive journey through the enchanting landscapes and rich cultural tapestry of Madeira, I am filled with an overwhelming sense of gratitude for having been a witness to the soul-stirring beauty that this island generously unveils. Madeira, with its dramatic cliffs, lush greenery, and vibrant festivals, has a way of capturing not just your attention but your heart.

A Symphony of Senses: Embracing the Island's Essence

In concluding this guide, I want to emphasize that Madeira is not merely a destination; it's an immersive experience, a symphony of senses that transcends the pages of a guidebook. The scent of blooming flowers in Funchal's botanical gardens, the taste of succulent passion fruits picked fresh from the vine, the sight of the sun dipping below the horizon, painting the sky with hues of orange and pink – these are the moments that linger in your memory, making Madeira a destination unlike any other.

Insider Tips: Navigating the Island Like a Local

For those eager to embrace Madeira's magic, here are some insider tips to enrich your journey:

- Dive into Local Cuisine: Don't miss the chance to savor the local delicacies. Indulge in the iconic Espetada, relish the flavors of the traditional Bolo do Caco, and pair it all with a glass of Madeira wine. The island's culinary scene is a journey in itself.

- Venture Beyond Funchal: While Funchal is a treasure trove of experiences, explore the lesser-known gems of Madeira. Visit the charming villages of São Vicente, Santana, and Ponta do Sol to witness the authentic island life and hospitality.

- Chase the Festivals: Time your visit to coincide with the island's vibrant festivals. Whether it's the lively Carnival of Funchal or the soulful Festival of São João, these celebrations offer a glimpse into the heart and soul of Madeira.

- Embark on a Levada Walk: Lace up your hiking boots and traverse the island's intricate network of levadas. These irrigation channels not only offer stunning views but also lead you to hidden waterfalls and secluded valleys, unveiling the raw, untouched beauty of Madeira.

- Witness a Sunset in Porto Moniz: Head to Porto Moniz on the northwest coast for a sunset like no other. The natural rock pools, carved by the relentless Atlantic waves, provide a dramatic backdrop as the sun dips below the horizon, casting a golden glow over the volcanic landscapes.

- Engage with Locals: The warmth of Madeiran hospitality is unparalleled. Strike up conversations with locals, participate in a traditional festival dance, or join a communal grape harvest. The connections you forge with the people of Madeira will leave an indelible mark on your travel experience.

A Final Note: Madeira, Forever in Your Heart

As you close the pages of this guide and contemplate your Madeira adventure, I urge you to approach the island with an open heart. Let its natural wonders captivate you, its festivals enliven your spirit, and its people embrace you. Madeira is not just a destination; it's a feeling, an emotion that stays with you long after you've bid farewell to its shores.

For the veteran traveler, the seeker of authenticity, and the lover of first-hand experiences, Madeira beckons you with open arms. It invites you to step beyond the ordinary, to immerse yourself in a world where every sunrise brings new possibilities and every sunset whispers tales of centuries-old traditions. As you venture into the heart of Madeira, may you find not just a destination but a lifelong connection to an island that etches itself onto your soul – an island that will forever hold a special place in the tapestry of your travel adventures.

So, my fellow wanderer, pack your bags, let curiosity guide your footsteps, and allow Madeira to unfold its wonders before you. In the words of Madeira's timeless allure, "Venha descobrir o encanto da Madeira" – come discover the enchantment of Madeira. The island awaits, ready to share its magic with you. Safe travels and may your journey be as extraordinary as the destination itself.

Copyrighted Material   **TARA'S LOCAL INSIGHT**

MADEIRA TRAVEL PLANNER AND 2024 CALENDAR

THIS TRAVEL PLANNER BELONGS TO

NAME:

WHY DO I WANT TO VISIT MADEIRA?

HOW LONG DO YOU INTEND STAYING IN MADEIRA?

WHAT IS YOUR ACCOMMODATION BUDGET?

WHAT IS YOUR TRAVEL BUDGET GENERALLY?

MY PACKING LIST

A-7 DAY TRAVEL ITINERARIES PLANNING

DAY 1:

DAY 2:

DAY 3:

DAY 4:

DAY 5:

DAY 6:

DAY 7:

TOP MUST-DO THINGS IN MADEIRA

MUST-TRY FOOD IN MADEIRA

MY MADEIRA TRAVEL BUDGET

LIST OF TOURIST SITES TO VISIT IN MADEIRA

SHARE YOUR MADEIRA TRAVEL EXPERIENCE

TARA'S LOCAL INSIGHT

2024 Calendar

JANUARY						
S	M	T	W	T	F	S
	1	2	3	4	5	6
7	8	9	10	11	12	13
14	15	16	17	18	19	20
21	22	23	24	25	26	27
28	29	30	31			

FEBRUARY						
S	M	T	W	T	F	S
				1	2	3
4	5	6	7	8	9	10
11	12	13	14	15	16	17
18	19	20	21	22	23	24
25	26	27	28	29		

MARCH						
S	M	T	W	T	F	S
					1	2
3	4	5	6	7	8	9
10	11	12	13	14	15	16
17	18	19	20	21	22	23
24	25	26	27	28	29	30
31						

APRIL						
S	M	T	W	T	F	S
	1	2	3	4	5	6
7	8	9	10	11	12	13
14	15	16	17	18	19	20
21	22	23	24	25	26	27
28	29	30				

MAY						
S	M	T	W	T	F	S
			1	2	3	4
5	6	7	8	9	10	11
12	13	14	15	16	17	18
19	20	21	22	23	24	25
26	27	28	29	30	31	

JUNE						
S	M	T	W	T	F	S
						1
2	3	4	5	6	7	8
9	10	11	12	13	14	15
16	17	18	19	20	21	22
23	24	25	26	27	28	29
30						

JULY						
S	M	T	W	T	F	S
	1	2	3	4	5	6
7	8	9	10	11	12	13
14	15	16	17	18	19	20
21	22	23	24	25	26	27
28	29	30	31			

AUGUST						
S	M	T	W	T	F	S
				1	2	3
4	5	6	7	8	9	10
11	12	13	14	15	16	17
18	19	20	21	22	23	24
25	26	27	28	29	30	31

SEPTEMBER						
S	M	T	W	T	F	S
1	2	3	4	5	6	7
8	9	10	11	12	13	14
15	16	17	18	19	20	21
22	23	24	25	26	27	28
29	30					

OCTOBER						
S	M	T	W	T	F	S
		1	2	3	4	5
6	7	8	9	10	11	12
13	14	15	16	17	18	19
20	21	22	23	24	25	26
27	28	29	30	31		

NOVEMBER						
S	M	T	W	T	F	S
					1	2
3	4	5	6	7	8	9
10	11	12	13	14	15	16
17	18	19	20	21	22	23
24	25	26	27	28	29	30

DECEMBER						
S	M	T	W	T	F	S
1	2	3	4	5	6	7
8	9	10	11	12	13	14
15	16	17	18	19	20	21
22	23	24	25	26	27	28
29	30	31				

Dear Travel Companions,

I hope this note finds you well, perhaps with a touch of wanderlust in your hearts. As the author of the "Madeira Comprehensive Travel Guide 2024 and Beyond," I am reaching out with immense gratitude for allowing me to share the wonders of Madeira with you. Our journey together doesn't end with the turning of the last page; it extends into the realm of shared experiences and cherished memories.

Being a veteran traveler and a passionate author, my greatest joy lies in weaving tales that inspire and guide fellow explorers. Crafting the "Madeira Comprehensive Travel Guide" was a labor of love, fueled by the belief that firsthand experiences and authentic knowledge are the true architects of an enriching travel narrative.

Now, as I extend this humble request, I want you to know that your thoughts, your feedback, and your connection mean the world to me. If, in any way, my guide has added a spark to your Madeiran adventures, or if you found a helpful nugget of information that made your journey more memorable, I kindly ask for a moment of your time.

Your reviews, like postcards from faraway lands, hold immense value. They not only validate the effort poured into the guide but also serve as beacons for fellow travelers seeking a roadmap to their own Madeira escapades. Your words have the power to create a community bound by shared stories, tips, and the sheer joy of exploration.

Leaving a positive review on Amazon and awarding those precious five stars is more than a gesture; it's a way of paying it forward to fellow explorers who are yet to embark on their Madeiran odyssey. Your generosity in sharing your experiences helps build a collective reservoir of knowledge, making the travel community richer and more vibrant.

Think of your review as a ripple in a vast ocean; its effects extend far beyond what meets the eye. It's a gift that keeps on giving, guiding and inspiring others to create their own Madeira stories. Your voice, your perspective, and your reflections matter—they breathe life into the guide, making it a living, evolving companion for every reader.

In the spirit of our shared love for discovery, I invite you to be a part of this journey not just as a reader but as a contributor to the tapestry of wanderlust. Your support fuels the passion for exploration that brought us together in the first place.

As we navigate the uncharted territories of Madeira and beyond, let our connection be more than just a fleeting chapter in your travel adventures. Let it be a lasting bond, woven with the threads of shared experiences and the echoes of your stories resonating through the travel community.

Thank you for being a vital part of this journey. Your kindness, your feedback, and your willingness to share the love for travel mean more to me than words can express. Here's to the magic of Madeira, the beauty of exploration, and the incredible community of fellow wanderers like you.

With heartfelt gratitude and the warmest of wishes,

[TARA WARREN]

Author, "Madeira Comprehensive Travel Guide 2024 and Beyond"

Printed in Great Britain
by Amazon